INTEGRITY

Examining How I Live

Center for Christian Leadership at Dallas Theological Seminary

NAVPRESS®

BRINGING TRUTH TO LIFE

OUR GUARANTEE TO YOU

The Navigators is an international Christian organization. Our mission is to reach, disciple, and equip people to know Christ and to make Him known through successive generations. We envision multitudes of diverse people in the United States and every other nation who have a passionate love for Christ, live a lifestyle of sharing Christ's love, and multiply spiritual laborers among those without Christ.

NavPress is the publishing ministry of The Navigators. NavPress publications help believers learn biblical truth and apply what they learn to their lives and ministries. Our mission is to stimulate spiritual formation among our readers.

© 2004 by Center for Christian Leadership

ISBN 1-57683-561-8

Cover design by Arvid Wallen
Creative Team: Jay Howver, Karen Lee-Thorp, Cara Iverson, Glynese Northam

Some of the anecdotal illustrations in this book are true to life and are included with the permission of the persons involved. All other illustrations are composites of real situations, and any resemblance to people living or dead is coincidental.

All Scripture quotations in this publication are taken from the HOLY BIBLE: NEW INTERNATIONAL VERSION® (NIV®). Copyright © 1973, 1978, 1984 by International Bible Society. Used by permission of Zondervan Publishing House. All rights reserved; the *New English Translation* (NET). Copyright © 2001 by Biblical Studies Press, L.L.C. www.netbible.com. All rights reserved; and the *New American Standard Bible* (NASB), © The Lockman Foundation 1960, 1962, 1963, 1968, 1971, 1972, 1973, 1975, 1977, 1995.

Printed in Canada

1 2 3 4 5 6 7 8 9 10 / 08 07 06 05 04

FOR A FREE CATALOG OF
NAVPRESS BOOKS & BIBLE STUDIES,
CALL 1-800-366-7788 (USA)
OR 1-416-499-4615 (CANADA)

Dallas Theological Seminary provided the context and the resources necessary for this series. Many students have given valuable feedback in the development at various stages. The support of the seminary administration has been invaluable. This series could not have come into being without its support.

WILLIAM G. MILLER
Resource Development Coordinator
Center for Christian Leadership
Dallas Theological Seminary

Acknowledgments

The TRANSFORMING LIFE series is based on a curriculum developed at Dallas Theological Seminary for its Spiritual Formation program, under the guidance of the Center for Christian Leadership. Hundreds of seminary students have benefited from this material, and now this adapted version makes it available to local churches and ministries.

This series would not have been possible without the contributions of many people and the support of Dallas Theological Seminary. The person primarily responsible for this series is Erik Petrik, senior pastor at Vail Bible Church in Vail, Colorado. As the director of the Spiritual Formation program in the late 1990s through 2000, Erik and his team developed the philosophy of this series and its fundamental components. The team he gathered included men and women with great spiritual insight and extensive ministry experience. It was primarily due to Erik's vision and the team's refining, researching, and writing that this series came to life.

In addition, the following persons made significant contributions: Terry Boyle, Barry Jones, Tim Lundy, Tom Miller, Elizabeth Nash, Jim Neathery, Kim Poupart, Kari Stainback, Troy Stringfield, and Monty Waldron. It was my great pleasure to work with each of them and experience the image of Christ in them.

Others who shaped the Spiritual Formation program at Dallas Seminary from the early 1990s are John Contoveros, Pete Deison, Martin Hironaga, David Kanne, Dr. Bill Lawrence, Brad Smith, and David Ward. Special appreciation goes to Pete Deison and David Kanne for their early contribution to what eventually became Life Story, and to Dr. Bill Lawrence, who gave the team the freedom to "think outside the box" when he was the executive director of the Center for Christian Leadership. Dr. Andrew Seidel, the current acting executive director, has continued to provide needed support through the process of revising the series for use in churches and ministries. Kerri Gupta contributed much time and energy cleaning up the manuscript. Thanks to her for her editing work.

Table of Contents

A Model of Spiritual Transformation

What's the first thing that comes to mind when you think of spiritual growth? Some picture a solitary individual meditating or praying. While that concept accurately portrays one aspect of Christian spirituality, it doesn't tell the whole story.

Three Aspects of Transformation

The issue of spiritual transformation is not new in the Christian faith. It has been a primary issue, though perhaps given different labels, throughout church history. From the time the Spirit of God descended upon the believers in Jerusalem, God has been transforming the souls of individual believers in the context of local Christian communities.

Preaching has never been and never will be the only element needed for the transformation of Christians into Christ's image. Nor are small-group Bible studies, personal Bible study, Sunday school classes, or even one-on-one discipleship sufficient for growing Christians when they focus solely on communicating biblical information. Therefore, a movement has grown that emphasizes transformation of the believer's inner and outer life and not just transformation of the intellect. Three broad approaches to spiritual transformation have developed.

Fellowship Model

One approach is to create fellowship opportunities. Churches develop structured settings for members to build relationships with others. They may launch small groups that meet in homes. They may convert their Sunday school classes into times of social engagement. These groups enable believers to be intimately involved in one another's lives. The fellowship model focuses on corporate prayer for one another, growth of interpersonal intimacy, and support for each other in times of need. This approach effectively connects believers within a church body.

Spiritual Disciplines Model

A second approach emphasizes disciplines such as meditation, prayer, fasting, and solitude. Such writers as Dallas Willard and Richard Foster have done excellent work on spiritual disciplines. This approach takes seriously the inner life and intimacy with God. However, when used in isolation, this approach can make people think spiritual transformation is a private matter. Even though the spiritual disciplines include communal elements (worship, service, and fellowship), some people treat the private exercises (silent retreats, journaling, meditating on Scripture, prayer, and fasting) as primary. That's a mistake.

Counseling Model

The third approach relies heavily on personal introspection. Christian counseling emphasizes areas of surrounding sin or personal character flaws that cause interpersonal problems or destructive behavior. Counseling seeks to understand the roots of such problems by looking at one's heritage and temperament. Usually in one-on-one interaction, the counselor probes for the root issues hidden beneath the surface problem. Discovering these deeper issues can shed light on a person's consistent failure to make wise choices. This approach focuses on identifying and dealing with those internal obstacles that prevent spiritual growth. Dealing with the issues is a key component in spiritual transformation.

The TRANSFORMING LIFE Model — An Integrated Approach

The three approaches are all valuable, but when taken alone they each have weaknesses. The fellowship model can fail to guide believers toward growth. The spiritual disciplines model can neglect to emphasize authentic and intimate Christian community, which is necessary for growth. The counseling model can fail to value the role that spiritual disciplines can have in growth. It also risks focusing on deficiencies so much that the person never benefits from the resources of God's grace. It can focus too intently upon the person's sin and failure and not enough on God's enabling power toward growth in holiness.

Therefore, TRANSFORMING LIFE brings in elements from all three approaches. The series tries to balance the inward and outward elements of spiritual transformation. Its theme is:

> Experiencing divine power through relationships;
> Striving together toward maturity in Christ.

We believe a particular context is essential to the transformation process. That context is authentic community in which people come to trust each other. Though one-on-one relationships can be effective, we believe that multiple relationships are more effective. While one individual can spur another toward growth, that one individual has limited gifts and abilities. Also, though we value the spiritual disciplines, we see them as means toward the end of complete transformation of the believer's inner and outer life. Disciplines aren't ends in themselves. Finally, we think believers need to seek greater understanding of sin's dynamic in their lives. They need to see potential blind spots or obstacles to their spiritual well-being and learn to deal with the root issues beneath their areas of struggle.

Our working definition of the Christian's transformation is:

> The process by which God forms Christ's character in believers by the ministry of the Spirit, in the context of community, and in accordance with biblical standards. This process involves the transformation of the whole person in thoughts, behaviors, and styles of relating with God and others. It results in a life of service to others and witness for Christ.

While the transformation process is an end in itself, the ultimate end is Christ's glory. He is the One adored by those who experience His presence and are transformed by Him. They, in turn, seek to exalt Him in the world.

Because each person is unique, God's formative process is unique for each. And though the Spirit of God is the One who transforms souls, each individual has personal responsibility in the process. Many spiritual disciplines can contribute, yet God is primarily concerned with transforming the whole person, not just patterns of behavior. For this reason, no one method (be it a traditional spiritual discipline or another method) is the single critical component.

TRANSFORMING LIFE depends solely on peer leadership. Groups don't need to be led by trained ministers. Leaders are more like facilitators—they don't need to have all the answers because group members learn from each other. The leader's role is to create an environment that fosters growth and encouragement.

Still, all small-group ministries need consistent coaching for the lay leaders. The group leaders need ministers and pastors to train and encourage them. A small-group ministry will raise all sorts of issues for leaders to deal with as people become honest about their lives in a trusting community. A group leader may need guidance about how to respond to a group member who shares that he has been having an e-mail "affair" and has not told his wife. Another may feel discouraged when group members drop out. Still another may wonder how to deal with two group members who are consistently angry with each other. It's important to provide support to those who take the risk to develop such an authentic environment for growth.

The Four Themes of This Series

Instead of aiming for competency in a set of skills or techniques, this series helps people identify the areas that must be developed in a believer's life. In other words, while it's necessary for a believer to know the "how-tos" of the Christian life, it's not sufficient. Knowing how to do personal Bible study and how to share Christ with others are praiseworthy skills. Developing these skills, however, is not the end goal but the means by which we live out who we are as new creatures in Christ. That's why this series addresses four critical components of the Christian life: identity, community, integrity, and ministry.

This series proposes that the Christian life involves:

> knowing your identity in Christ
> *so that*
> you can make yourself known to others in a Christian community
> *so that*
> you can pursue a lifetime of growth in the context of community
> *so that*
> you are best equipped to glorify Christ by serving others.

Identity

To understand our need for transformation, we must understand who we are currently, both as individuals and as members of the body of Christ. Who we are has undoubtedly been shaped by our past. Therefore, we explore various aspects of our identity, such as our heritage and temperament. What do these tell us about who we are and what we value? The interaction during this study bonds us and builds trust among us. Our goal is not to analyze, criticize, or control each other, but it is to grow and affirm what God is doing in and through one another.

In *Identity*, we ultimately want group members to see themselves in light of their identity in Christ. However, many of the values we actually live out stem from such influences as temperament, family background, and culture. Not all of those values are contrary to our new identity in Christ. For example, the value one person places on honesty, which he learned from his parents, is affirmed by his identity in Christ.

It can take a long time—more than a lifetime allows—for the Spirit of God to transform our values to line up with our new identity in Christ. We cooperate with the Spirit when we reflect on what our values are and how well they line up with our identity in Christ as described in Scripture.

One of the most significant characteristics of our identity in Christ is that we are now part of the body of Christ. The Christian life cannot be lived in isolation.

Community

So, while talking about *my* place in Christ, I need to pay attention to *our* place in Christ as a community. Understanding our corporate identity in Christ is crucial for a healthy community transformation process. The *Community* study helps a group not only understand how a Christian community develops but also experience a growing sense of community.

In order to experience intimate community in the biblical sense, we must learn to reveal ourselves to others. We need to honestly, freely, and thoughtfully tell our stories. Our modern culture makes it easy for people to live isolated and anonymous lives. Because we and others move frequently, we may feel it's not worth the effort to be vulnerable in short-lived relationships. However, we desperately need to keep intentionally investing in significant relationships.

Real involvement in others' lives requires more than what the term *fellowship* has too often come to mean. Real involvement includes holding certain values in common and practicing a lifestyle we believe is noble, while appreciating that this lifestyle doesn't make us perfect. Rather, this lifestyle is a commitment to let God continue to spiritually form us.

Community includes a group exercise, "Life Story," that has been tremendously effective in building community and enhancing self-understanding. "Life Story" walks a person through the process of putting together a personal, creative presentation of the most formative relationships and experiences of his or her life. As people share their stories with each other, a deep level of trust and commitment grows.

Integrity

By the time a group has experienced *Identity* and *Community* together, members have built significant intimacy and trust. Now they're ready to pursue a harder step. It's the heart of our approach to spiritual transformation. Many believers greatly underestimate the necessity of intimacy and trust for successful growth in Christian holiness. But we must be able to share honestly those areas in which we need transformation. We can deal with deep issues of growth only in a community in which we're deeply known by others. We need others who have our best interests at heart. They must also be people we trust to hold sensitive issues in genuine confidence.

Why does the pursuit of Christian holiness need to occur in community? There are at least two reasons. First, we need accountability in the areas of sin with which we struggle. When we confess our struggles to a group, we become accountable to all of the members to press on toward growth. Because the group is aware of our sin, we can't hide it in darkness, where it retains a hold on our life and can make crippling guilt a permanent fixture in our walk. If we're struggling, we have not one but several people to lean on. In addition, the corporate, or group, setting increases the likelihood of support from someone else who has struggled in the same way. In one-on-one accountability, one person may not be able to relate well to the other's struggles. He or she may have different areas of struggle.

The second benefit of corporate pursuit of holiness is that without the encouragement and stimulus of other Christians, we're often blind to the ways in which we need to grow. In the counsel of many who care for us, there can be greater wisdom. If some believers are blind to being hospitable, the hospitality of another believer can spur them on to develop that quality in their own lives. If some never think about how to speak encouraging words, the encouraging speech of another can become contagious.

Ministry

With *Identity*, *Community*, and *Integrity* as a foundation, believers are prepared to discern how God wants them to serve in the body of Christ. "Where can I serve?" is not an optional question; every believer should ask it. Nor is this a matter simply for individual reflection. Rather, we can best discern where and how to serve while in community with people who know our past, interests, struggles, and talents. The community can affirm what they see in us and may know of opportunities to serve that we're unaware of.

How many terrific musicians are sitting in pews every Sunday because they lack the confidence to volunteer? Those gifted people might merely need others who know them well to encourage them to serve. Maybe someone's life story revealed that while growing up she played in a band. Someone might ask, "What have you done with that interest lately?"

The Layout of *Integrity*

Each session contains the following elements:
- *Session Aims* states a goal for you as an individual and one for the group.
- Preparation tells what assignment(s) you need to complete ahead of time in order to get the most out of the group. For this study, much of the preparation will involve completing "Life Change" exercises. The "Life Change" exercises can be found on pages 73-121.
- *Introduction* sets up the session's topic.
- *Content* provides material around which group discussions and exercises will focus. You should read the "Introduction" and "Content" sections before your group meeting so you'll be prepared to discuss them.

- *Conclusion* wraps up the session and sets the scene for the next one.
- *Assignment* lists "homework" to complete before the next session meeting.

In this way, each session includes all three aspects of transformation: personal introspection, spiritual disciplines, and the experience of God in relationships. Through all of these means, the Spirit of God will be at work in your life.

A Method for the Biblical Exercises

The biblical exercises will guide you through a self-study of a passage that relates to the session topic. You'll begin by making observations about the passage. Pay attention to the following categories:

Who?

Identify persons in the passage: the description of persons, the relationships between persons, and the condition of persons.

What?

Identify subjects in the passage: the issues or topics being addressed.

When?

Identify time in the passage: duration of time that passes and when the events occurred in relationship to one another.

Where?

Identify places in the passage: the descriptions of locations, the relationships of places to other places, and the relationships of persons to the places.

Why?

Identify purposes in the passage: the expressions of purpose by the author and/or the characters.

How?

Identify events in the passage: the descriptions of events unfolding, the relationships between events, and the order of events.

In *Living By the Book*, Dr. Howard Hendricks and William Hendricks identify six categories that aid the process of observation. They encourage readers to "look for things that are (1) emphasized, (2) repeated, (3) related, (4) alike, (5) unlike, or (6) true to life."[1]

After you make observations, you will interpret the passage. Interpretation involves determining what the main point of the passage is. Then you'll reflect on how the main point applies to your life. Be sure to ask for God's guidance in your reflection. After all, the purpose of Scripture is for God to speak to us and, as a result, for our lives to be transformed.

Christian Integrity and Community

You and your small group are about to study Christian integrity. It makes sense, then, to ask, "Why do we need to be in a group in order to deal with integrity? Can't we simply hear preaching, study our Scriptures, ask for assistance in private prayer, and exert our own willpower to pursue holiness? What role does a community play in our pursuit of holiness?" This session will address those questions. The entire study, with its group exercises, will help you experience community's essential role in your growth in integrity.

Session Aims

Individual Aim: To consider why you need community for your pursuit of holiness.

Group Aim: To discuss community's role in contributing to a person's growth in integrity.

Preparation

Read *Session 1: Christian Integrity and Community.*

Complete *Biblical Exercise: Ephesians 4* beginning on page 19.

Introduction

In North American culture, individualism and independence reign. However, the New Testament describes Christian community as *inter*dependent. Interdependence involves mutual encouragement and intimacy.

Interdependent *Christian* community also includes a commitment to holiness. Though our culture affirms some of the positive benefits of community, it often balks at the uniquely Christian commitment to holiness in community. It sees as "cultish" communities that want members to be mutually accountable to each other for some definite ethical standard.

It's no surprise, then, that many churches seem to endorse a very private pursuit of holiness. Yet the New Testament presents a community in which the members have a mutual responsibility to one another in their pursuit of holiness. The members of local churches need to help each other grow in godliness.

Content

When asked, "Do you want to live more and more like Jesus every day?" most Christians would say "yes." But if believers cognitively assent to a desire to grow in Christlikeness, why do so many struggle to see such growth in day-to-day living? What is missing?

In many cases, believers who struggle to grow have a healthy dose of biblical input from over four dozen Sunday sermons annually, supplemented by Christian radio, Sunday school classes, or Wednesday night church services. But are our lives really changed simply by exposing our intellects to more information?

We have been trained to share the Christian message effectively with others, taught how to develop a regular prayer life, and equipped to minister to those in need. We understand that many Christian activities must occur in a corporate, or group, setting. So why do we seldom understand our growth toward Christlikeness, our sanctification, as a communal endeavor? This study will not simply expose you to principles that help you better understand what moral wholeness, or integrity, looks like in the Christian life; it will also encourage you to engage in the process of growth with others.

> It must be remembered, first of all, that we are not sanctified merely as individuals but as members of the body of Christ. . . . We must therefore live in such a way as to advance and enrich the sanctification of the fellow believers whom our lives touch.
> —Anthony A. Hoekema, *Saved by Grace*[1]

> Growth in true holiness is always growth together; it takes place through the nurture, the work and worship of the church.
> —Edmund P. Clowney, *The Church: Contours of Christian Theology*[2]

Believers often mistakenly assume that growing in holiness is simply a matter of either exerting personal willpower or passively expecting God to act. But even those who understand the need for both exerting one's will and developing dependence on Christ still need the encouraging support of a community of other Christians—at least that is what Jesus and His apostles had in mind.

Paul consistently described a corporate dynamic of growth (Romans 15:14; 2 Corinthians 1:4; 1 Thessalonians 4:18; 5:11,14; 2 Thessalonians 3:11-15; Titus 1:9; 2:4,15). Paul never imagined sanctification of isolated individuals but always of individuals within the context of an intimate community.

For a powerful example of the kind of community believers ought to experience, consider one of Jesus' final prayers on earth. In John 17:20-23, Jesus says He desires believers to have the same intimacy with one another as He and the Father share. One significant reason for that level of intimacy is the encouragement it provides for growth. In that kind of supporting—and at times correcting—community, believers help each other so that their active living is saturated with the principles of Christian integrity.

Conclusion

Participating in this study with a group of fellow believers is no trivial commitment. If you are unwilling to corporately confess your own sin and commit to pursue growth in new ways, this may not be the study for you. However, if you are willing, even if fearfully willing, to enter into this process, you will find yourself not only supported in your struggle against sinful influences but also given a renewed vision and motivation for pursuing holiness.

Biblical Exercise: Ephesians 4

Read Ephesians 4:1-16. Also, review "A Method for the Biblical Exercises" beginning on page 15.

Observation — **"What Do I See?"**

1. Who are the persons (including God) in the passage? What is the condition of those persons?

2. What subjects did Paul discuss in the passage? What did he assert?

3. Note the sequence in which Paul made these assertions. (You might number them in order.)

4. What did Paul emphasize? Are there repeated ideas and themes? How are the various parts related?

5. Why did Paul write this passage? (Did he say anything about ways he expected the reader to change after reading it?)

Interpretation Phase 1 — "What Did It Mean Then?"

1. Coming to Terms—Are there any words in the passage that you don't understand? Write down anything you found confusing about the passage.

2. Finding Where It Fits—What clues does the Bible give about the meaning of this passage?

   - Immediate Context (the passage being studied)

   - Remote Context (passages that come before and after the one being studied)

3. Getting into Their Sandals—An Exercise in Imagination

   - What are the main points of this passage? Summarize or write an outline of it.

   - What do you think the recipients of the letter were supposed to take from this passage? How did God, inspiring Paul to write Ephesians, want this passage to impact the Ephesian believers?

Interpretation Phase 2—**"What Does It Mean Now?"**

1. What is the timeless truth in the passage? In one or two sentences, write down what you learned about God from Ephesians 4.

2. How does that truth work today?

Application—**"What Can I Do to Make This Truth Real?"**

1. What can I do to make this truth real for myself?

2. For my family?

3. For my friends?

4. For the people who live near me?

5. For the rest of the world?

Assignment

Read *Session 2: Belief and Practice.*

Complete the *Life Change: Belief and Practice* exercise beginning on page 75.

Belief and Practice

We want to be men and women of integrity with the Lord, in our homes, with our friends, and in the workplace. But what does that mean? This session will help us get a better grasp on the term *integrity*.

> *integrity:* (1) soundness of and adherence to moral principle and character; uprightness; honesty; (2) the state of being whole, entire, or undiminished: to preserve the integrity of the empire; (3) a sound, unimpaired, or perfect condition: the integrity of the text; the integrity of a ship's hull[1]

To have integrity is to live and think according to a standard of truth, which is God's character as revealed in His Word. Integrity involves wholeness or soundness. It is more than abiding by a list of dos and don'ts. It involves loving God in our hearts by affirming His standards in our minds through godly living with our bodies. Integrity involves a commitment to self-scrutiny to determine whether our affirmed beliefs match our daily lives.

Session Aims

Individual Aim: To recognize the disparity between the biblical beliefs you hold and what you practice in daily life.

Group Aim: To discuss the challenge of living consistently by biblically grounded beliefs and to be encouraged by past examples of growth.

Preparation

Read *Session 2: Belief and Practice.*

Read the *Life Change: Belief and Practice* exercise beginning on page 75.

Introduction

> It is not excess of thought but defect of fertile and generous emotion that marks [many intellectuals] out. Their heads are no bigger than the ordinary; it is the atrophy of the chest beneath that makes them seem so.
>
> —C. S. Lewis, *The Abolition of Man*[2]

Sometimes gaining more information about God and the Christian life can be oppressive. If that statement seems strange, consider a consequence of acquiring such knowledge. One major consequence is that learning brings a greater responsibility to live according to that knowledge. If we take our growth seriously, we can leave our sanctuaries many Sunday mornings burdened by an understanding of a new biblical principle that we feel obliged to practice in our lives. The more clearly we understand God's holiness and His expectation that we become like Him in holiness, the more the pursuit of holiness can seem an overwhelming task. Yet Jesus said that His "yoke is easy" and His "burden is light" (Matthew 11:30).

Though following Jesus certainly involves a yoke and a burden, it is not meant to be overwhelming. As we look at the inner workings of our lives, remember that our Master is "gentle and humble in heart" (Matthew 11:29). If we remember the grace He bestowed upon us by granting us forgiveness, we will experience that grace anew as we honestly see our heart condition. In addition, we may be surprised to see how dramatically our Master has already transformed us from the time we placed our faith in Him.

Content

Theologians use the term *sanctification* to describe the process whereby Christians become set apart from the world's ways of thinking and behaving. Sanctification is how Christians grow in holiness. It describes how, for example, a person who approaches life with an attitude of "win at all costs" is transformed into a person who can turn the other cheek. Sanctification is all about life change.

However, if we honestly evaluate our lives, we might find that though we have beliefs about how to live the Christian life, we do not always practice them. While we won't list in this session all the biblical beliefs that ought to guide our daily practice, we must recognize the importance of biblically grounded beliefs and evaluate our own. The Savior commissioned the apostles to teach new converts "to obey everything I have commanded you" (Matthew 28:20). Jesus doesn't want us to conform to an ethic generated by the world and our own creativity. Our standard is what is laid down in Scripture, not what we fancy or what the world affirms:

> *Do not conform any longer to the pattern of this world, but be transformed by the renewing of your mind. Then you will be able to test and approve what God's will is—his good, pleasing and perfect will.* (Romans 12:2)

Life change begins in our minds. Scripture reveals to us the beliefs we should profess.

The second step is equally significant. It is no easy task to practice what we believe, because the world operates by different standards. In addition, practicing biblical beliefs in the midst of a fluid and complex world is enormously challenging. Often, our biblical beliefs don't adequately permeate our thoughts, attitudes, and behaviors in the course of a day. What we really value at any moment is expressed not exclusively by the beliefs we affirm but also by how we react or respond to our life events, role models, and cultural background—by the strategies we use to cope with life as a whole. We usually live by a mixture of principles acquired from sermons, Bible study, and fellowship, along with approaches we've acquired from what the Bible calls "the world" and "the flesh."

Our past life experience and our culture often hinder us from practicing our beliefs more fully. For example, even though a believer may intellectually understand that God is faithful, if he never experienced consistent care and protection from his own father, he may operate as if God is not trustworthy to provide for his basic needs. Instead of trusting God during a financial crisis, he may react to the crisis with overwhelming anxiety and decide to compromise his Christian business ethics.

Conclusion

No matter how biblically accurate our beliefs are, head knowledge alone cannot make us holy, because our hearts still hold to the patterns of the flesh (Jeremiah 17:9; Romans 7:14-23; James 1:15; 1 John 1:8). Even though we know we are utterly dependent upon God for life, we all try to manage our lives independently of God at some times and to varying degrees. To understand more deeply why we fail to live by our beliefs, in the next session we will look at the biblical concept of the flesh.

Lest we become too discouraged by the gap between our beliefs and practice, we should celebrate our progress with Christ thus far. By evaluating our past attempts at life change, we can better understand how we help and hinder God's sanctifying work in our lives.

Assignment

Read *Session 3: Flesh*.

Complete *Biblical Exercise: Romans 1* beginning on page 32.

Flesh

In the last session we recognized that practicing what we believe is hard. Why are we so prone to living contrary to what we say we believe? Scripture tells us that both the fallen world in which we live and our enemy, Satan, influence us to live contrary to biblical principles. But another major factor is what the apostle Paul calls our "flesh." We will examine the concept of the flesh to see what exactly the Scriptures mean by the term. We will also explore the way our struggle with the flesh shows itself in our lives.

Session Aims

Individual Aim: To examine the effects of an orientation toward self by considering both the overt and subtle manifestations of the flesh.

Group Aim: To recognize manifestations of the flesh that many group members share.

Preparation

Read *Session 3: Flesh*.

Complete *Biblical Exercise: Romans 1* beginning on page 32.

Introduction

In *The Divine Conspiracy*, Dallas Willard cites a Gallup survey indicating that 94 percent of Americans claim to believe in God, 74 percent claim to have made a commitment to Jesus Christ, and about 34 percent profess to have had a "new birth" experience. He then adds, "These figures are shocking when thoughtfully compared to statistics on the same group for unethical behavior, crime, mental distress and disorder, family failures, addictions, financial misdealings and the like. . . . Could such a combination of profession and failure really be the 'life and life abundantly' that Jesus said he came to give?"[1]

What could possibly account for such a disparity between profession and practice? We might suspect that many who make such claims are mistaken as to what a commitment to Christ is. But all of us can probably think of men and women who we think are genuine believers yet whose lives exhibit this same inconsistency. And in our moments of honest self-reflection, we recognize that often we don't need to look any further than our own hearts and lives to see the evidence of this disparity.

Content

Paul makes a clear distinction between those who "walk by the Spirit" and those who "carry out the desire of the flesh" (Galatians 5:16, NASB). "Flesh" in this passage is often understood as a reference to a sin nature that remains in the believer, doing battle with his new spiritual nature. (The NIV renders "flesh" as "sinful nature.")

However, such an explanation seems inconsistent with Paul's view of human nature. While Greeks in his day saw a dichotomy between the human body, which to them was inherently evil, and the soul, which was inherently good, Paul knew of no such dichotomy. Instead, as Scot McKnight explains,

> When Paul uses "flesh," he is not thinking primarily in terms of "body" and the inferiority of the body in comparison to the spiritual aspect of human nature. This is a Platonic notion, not a biblical one. What Paul has in mind is "the total person living outside of God's will and apart from God's guiding influence through the Spirit."[2]

For Paul then, sin is not restricted to one part of us. Nor is there another part of us that transcends sin's corruption. Rather, Paul sees that though we are redeemed people, we are still fallen people and part of a fallen creation. While we are no longer what we once were, we are not yet what we one day will be. It is not our nature but our allegiances that are divided. Our practice often fails to line up with our vow of faith because rather than submitting to and relying on the Spirit, we assert our self-sufficiency.

The conflict between the flesh and the Spirit is not between one part of us and another part of us but rather between us and the Holy Spirit of God. As Robert Pyne points out, "We continue to sin, but we cannot blame our struggle on a particular part of ourselves. . . . To do so would be to avoid full responsibility for our behavior, and that avoidance would only compound the problem."[3]

Anthony Thiselton defines the flesh like this: "The outlook of the flesh is the outlook oriented toward the self, that which pursues its own ends in self-sufficient independence of God."[4] Here is the reason we often fail to practice what we say we believe. We are born with this selfish disposition, our culture reinforces it, and it remains with us even after we are born again. We are all in the process of having our hearts transformed from an outlook oriented toward the self into an outlook oriented toward God and others. But part of the transformation involves recognizing our selfish disposition and submitting to God's will. Such recognition and submission does not come easily.

In Galatians 5:19-21 (NET), Paul identified the "works of the flesh" as "sexual immorality, impurity, depravity, idolatry, sorcery, hostilities, strife, jealousy, outbursts of anger, selfish rivalries, dissensions, factions, envying, murder, drunkenness, carousing, and similar things." These overt manifestations of the flesh can be summed up by two broad categories of motivation that express an outlook oriented toward the self: (1) the desire for control and power and (2) the desire for self-gratification. For example, those in Paul's day who practiced idolatry wanted gods they could control and use to gain power. Those involved in drunkenness used alcohol to gain self-gratification.

For those of us who have spent much time around the church, such overt manifestations of the outlook oriented toward the self may not be our primary struggles. But Paul's list is not intended to be exhaustive. Honest reflection will reveal that we all still have behaviors and attitudes, subtle or overt, that express our desire for control or self-gratification. We all still struggle with an outlook oriented toward the self.

Conclusion

Throughout Galatians 5, Paul spoke of Christian freedom, but Paul's understanding of Christian freedom did not mean self-sufficiency or autonomy. The quest to be self-sufficient and autonomous reflects the outlook oriented toward the self. Christian freedom means freedom from the law and the power of sin, but it also involves submission to God's will and dependence on His Spirit. Unfortunately, Christians can and often do make the illogical choice to behave as though they were self-sufficient and autonomous. Then they carry out the "works of the flesh." In calling Christians to "walk by the Spirit," Paul pointed out this irony: In dependence on the Spirit and in submission to God's will lies great freedom, while the assertion of one's self-sufficient independence brings only bondage.

Biblical Exercise: Romans 1

Read Romans 1:18-32. Also, review "A Method for the Biblical Exercises" beginning on page 15.

Observation — "What Do I See?"

1. Who are the persons (including God) in the passage? What is the condition of those persons?

2. What subjects did Paul discuss in the passage? What did he assert?

3. Note the sequence in which Paul made these assertions. (You might number them in order.)

4. What did Paul emphasize? Are there repeated ideas and themes? How are the various parts related?

5. Why did Paul write this passage? (Did he say anything about ways he expected the reader to change after reading it?)

Interpretation Phase 1 — **"What Did It Mean Then?"**

1. Coming to Terms—Are there any words in the passage that you don't understand? Write down anything you found confusing about the passage.

2. Finding Where It Fits—What clues does the Bible give about the meaning of this passage?

    • Immediate Context (the passage being studied)

    • Remote Context (passages that come before and after the one being studied)

3. Getting into Their Sandals—An Exercise in Imagination

    • What are the main points of this passage? Summarize or write an outline of it.

- What do you think the recipients of the letter were supposed to take from this passage? How did God, inspiring Paul to write Romans, want this passage to impact the Roman believers?

Interpretation Phase 2—"What Does It Mean Now?"

1. What is the timeless truth in the passage? In one or two sentences, write down what you learned about God from Romans 1.

2. How does that truth work today?

Application—"What Can I Do to Make This Truth Real?"

1. What can I do to make this truth real for myself?

2. For my family?

3. For my friends?

4. For the people who live near me?

5. For the rest of the world?

Assignment

Read *Session 4: Seven Deadly Sins.*

Complete the *Life Change: Seven Deadly Sins* exercise beginning on page 82.

Seven Deadly Sins

If we desire to pursue integrity wholeheartedly, we must be willing to acknowledge sin's presence in our lives. The next few sessions are designed to prompt honest assessment of where sin has taken root in us. We expect the Spirit to produce heartfelt conviction in areas of needed change—the kind of conviction that will lead to repentance. As a community, we are called to "confess [our] sins to each other" (James 5:16). In this session we will identify and share areas in which we are most likely to struggle with sin. This will prepare us for the following session, in which we each will write and present an assessment of how one area of sin affects us.

Session Aims

Individual Aim: To identify predominant areas of sin in your life and consider how those areas stem from issues of personal identity.

Group Aim: To share with one another your areas of greatest struggle and discuss how those areas stem from issues of personal identity.

Preparation

Read *Session 4: Seven Deadly Sins.*

Complete the *Life Change: Seven Deadly Sins* exercise beginning on page 82.

Introduction

The list known as the seven deadly sins (pride, envy, anger, greed, lust, sloth, gluttony) was used as early as the sixth century AD to help Christians identify and address the roots of sin in their lives. The list isn't meant to cover all sin or even the worst sins but rather seven foundational sins that underlie and nourish the rest.

Medieval theologian St. John of the Cross wrote that God digs out these seven root sins most deeply when believers enter a "dark night of the soul." John said such dark times are inevitable and are opportunities for growth because they force the believer to deal with areas of sin otherwise dormant in them. During such times, according to John, God removes some of the "consolations" the young believer has enjoyed. Young believers are like nursing babies who must mature in their faith, but the process of growth brings trials, including temptations to stumble in these seven ways. Yet while life brings such temptations, believers can be confident that God will remain diligent to continue His work of transformation:

> His love is not content to leave us in our weakness, and for this reason he takes us into a dark night. He weans us from all the pleasures [of the Christian life] by giving us dry times and inward darkness. In doing so he is able to take away all these [seven deadly] vices and create virtues within us. Through the dark night pride becomes humility, greed becomes simplicity, wrath becomes contentment, luxury becomes peace, gluttony becomes moderation, envy becomes joy, and sloth becomes strength.
>
> —St. John of the Cross[1]

Content

While categories help us identify areas of greatest struggle, they sometimes overlap. For example, pride is the most fundamental sin and is contained in all sin, as James states:

> "God opposes the proud
> but gives grace to the humble."

> Submit yourselves, then, to God. Resist the devil, and he will flee from you. Come near to God and he will come near to you. Wash your hands, you sinners, and purify your hearts, you double-minded. (James 4:6-8)

Every sin includes an attempt to attain a desire in ways that are contrary to God's purposes and His ways of attaining those purposes. Consider envy. If people desire others' recognition, they may spread gossip about someone they envy. Decreasing a competitor's reputation may seem like a means to increasing one's own reputation in comparison. In this case, the purpose (obtaining more recognition from others) and the means to that end (spreading gossip) are both contrary to God's will.

In contrast, consider gluttony. Eating and drinking are not contrary to God's will. However, the purpose that drives our desire to eat and drink can be. If we are eating and drinking excessively for the purpose of escaping hardships in life, we are gluttons. We should not substitute eating and drinking for dependence on God to sustain us through hardship. The purpose of eating and drinking is to sustain our bodies and, in some situations, to celebrate. (Feasts in the Old Testament and the "potlucks" of the early church [see Acts 2:42-47] show that celebration is a valid reason for eating and drinking.)

Most of the categories of sin occur in human relations. When a person struggles with greed, he desires some material thing that another person has. If he did not observe another person possessing that object, greed might never have sprung up. When a person struggles with anger, she typically is enraged at another person's actions or words. Therefore, interpersonal communication often plays a central role in sin and virtue. Lying is not on the list of seven deadly sins, perhaps because many of the sins involve deceptive communication. Deceptive communication includes blatant and subtle forms of lying as well as nonverbal communication. Suggestions can be made without words. For example, a person might want others to think he is grieving a coworker's failure, when in fact he envies his coworker. When he hears of that person's failure, he may use facial expressions that communicate sadness for the coworker, while inside he is secretly rejoicing.

In *The Inferno*,[2] Dante Alighieri describes the various levels of hell. In the deepest levels are those who engaged in what Dante calls *fraud*. Dante means *lying*, which is the use of communication to deceive others for personal gain or pleasure. The point is that though we may struggle with being deceptive in our communication with others, deception is usually only a means to some other end. There is some larger issue of sin driving that mode of communication.

Conclusion

It is difficult to face our sins honestly and even more difficult to share them honestly. The "Seven Deadly Sins" exercise and the sharing that will take place in the next two sessions are designed to help you identify not only some important areas of sin in your life but also some of the root causes. The exercise will require some thought and creativity, but it is worth the effort.

We must always guard against the temptations presented by our flesh, the world, and our spiritual enemy. But the struggle with sin is not the central focus of the Christian life. The Christian life is not chiefly about avoiding sin but about learning how to love God and people. Keep this in mind as you go through this part of the study.

Assignment

Read *Sessions 5 and 6: A Letter from Your Tempter.*

Complete the *Life Change: A Letter from Your Tempter* exercise beginning on page 96.

Half the group members should be prepared to share their tempter letters at the next group session.

A Letter from Your Tempter

In your last session, you began to share some of the main areas of sin in your life. Identifying those areas is one step in the process of confession. However, it is critical to move beyond that initial acknowledgment of sin to an examination of the inner dynamics of it.

Over the next two sessions, each group member will talk about how a particular sin issue affects his or her life, using the creative format of a letter from an imaginary personal demon as a means of opening communication and increasing vulnerability. This exercise will encourage you to think about how your specific sin operates, what payoff you hope for from the sin, and what habits and ways of thinking from our culture or your personal history the sin stems from.

Session Aims

Individual Aim: To share openly with the group one of the main sins you struggle with.

Group Aim: To experience mutual confession and encouragement.

Preparation

Read *Sessions 5 and 6: A Letter from Your Tempter.*

Complete the *Life Change: A Letter from Your Tempter* exercise beginning on page 96.

Half the group members should be prepared to share their tempter letters in session 5, while the rest should be prepared to share them in session 6.

Introduction

In his marvelous book *The Screwtape Letters*, C. S. Lewis used the correspondence between a supervising demon, Screwtape, and his young apprentice, Wormwood, to give a behind-the-scenes look at the machinations of evil. Readers get a glimpse of how evil conspires to work with a person's strengths and weaknesses in order to encourage moral and spiritual failure or at least to make the person live a baneful existence. The young demon is supposed to manipulate "his" human's desires and twist his efforts at love and wisdom so that they end up in sin or failure.

Content

In these two sessions, group members will read to one another their letters from their imagined tempters. (The corresponding "Life Change" exercise beginning on page 96 guides you through the writing of your letter.) Sharing the letters should be done in a single-sex setting. Select a second group leader for these two meetings.

The following verses provide helpful ground rules for this exercise:

> Brothers, if someone is caught in a sin, you who are spiritual should restore him gently. But watch yourself, or you also may be tempted. Carry each other's burdens, and in this way you will fulfill the law of Christ. If anyone thinks he is something when he is nothing, he deceives himself. Each one should test his own actions. Then he can take pride in himself, without comparing himself to somebody else, for each one should carry his own load. (Galatians 6:1-5)

Each member will read his or her tempter letter unless there is some exceptional circumstance. If you feel convicted against sharing about a certain area of struggle, choose another area to address in your letter. But think about that area you're unwilling to talk about with your group, and ask yourself, *Who do I feel comfortable sharing this with?* If you don't confess your areas of greatest struggle to someone, the secrecy of that sin and the bearing of that sin on your own may be giving that sin even more control over your life. Make sure that someone in your life whom you trust and respect is aware of that sin and can support you in overcoming that area.

Conclusion

The tempter letter exercise wraps up your exploration of sin. The other side of integrity is the positive pursuit of holiness. Exploring sin is defensive—with help from God and the community of believers, you try to avoid sinful behaviors or attitudes. Pursuing holiness is offensive—you don't guard against sin in order to be neutral but to learn to positively love God and others more intentionally and proactively. The rest of this study will address holiness. As a transition, you'll discuss how the fear of the Lord sustains both the defensive and offensive aspects of integrity.

Assignment

Read *Session 7: The Fear of the Lord.*

Complete *Biblical Exercise: Genesis 20 and 22* beginning on page 46.

The Fear of the Lord

"The fear of the LORD is the beginning of knowledge." (Proverbs 1:7)

Having addressed how sin works in our lives, we now turn to how we grow in holiness. Growth takes knowledge. When we talk about sanctification, we must emphasize knowledge. Sanctification is not a list of steps or self-help principles that we can check off. It calls for great knowledge to know how to walk with God through the diverse circumstances of life.

And to grow in knowledge, we need to fear the Lord; that is, to be whole, to be single-minded, and to live according to the biblical standard requires a continual process of learning who God is and realizing how desperate our situation is apart from Him.

In this session, keep in mind how a reverence for God helps you guard against failing in the areas of struggle you discussed in previous sessions and motivates you to pursue positive growth in holiness.

Session Aims

Individual Aim: To expand your understanding of and growth in the fear of the Lord.

Group Aim: To explore ways to incorporate an understanding of the fear of the Lord into the daily lives of group members.

Preparation

Read *Session 7: The Fear of the Lord.*

Complete *Biblical Exercise: Genesis 20 and 22* beginning on page 46.

Biblical Exercise: Genesis 20 and 22

Read Genesis 20; 22:1-19. Also, review "A Method for the Biblical Exercises" beginning on page 15.

Observation—"What Do I See?"

1. Who are the persons (including God) in the passage? What is the condition of those persons?

2. What are they saying or doing? (Look especially for statements or actions that are emphasized, repeated, related, alike, unalike, or true to life.)

3. When did this take place?

4. Where did this take place?

5. Why did it happen?

- What changed between the beginning and the end of chapter 20?

- What changed between the beginning and the end of chapter 22?

Interpretation Phase 1 — **"What Did It Mean Then?"**

1. Coming to Terms—Are there any words in the passage that you don't understand? Write down anything you found confusing about the passage.

2. Finding Where It Fits—What clues does the Bible give about the meaning of this passage?
   - Immediate Context (the passage being studied)

   - Remote Context (passages that come before and after the one being studied)

3. Getting into Their Sandals—An Exercise in Imagination
   - How did it look?

   - How did it sound?

   - How did it smell?

   - How did it feel?

   - How did it taste?

Interpretation Phase 2 — **"What Does It Mean Now?"**

1. What is the timeless truth in the passage? In one or two sentences, write down what you learned about God from Genesis 20 and 22.

2. How does that truth work today?

Application — **"What Can I Do to Make This Truth Real?"**

1. What can I do to make this truth real for myself?

2. For my family?

3. For my friends?

4. For the people who live near me?

5. For the rest of the world?

Introduction

When Abraham moved his family to the Negev region, he told residents there that his wife, Sarah, was his sister. The king of that region, Abimelech, took Sarah to become one of his wives. Before having Sarah as his wife, Abimelech had a dream in which God warned against it because she was Abraham's wife. Abraham admitted that the reason he lied about Sarah was because he thought, "There is surely no fear of God in this place, and they will kill me because of my wife" (Genesis 20:11).

Abraham knew that the people of the Negev had no knowledge of his God and did not live according to His standards. He assumed God could not or would not take care of him in such a place, so he took matters into his own hands by lying about Sarah's identity. The irony of the story is that Abraham was the one who showed that he didn't fear God.

The situation was different in Genesis 22. In this situation, many years later, Abraham showed his obedience to God in his willingness to sacrifice his son Isaac. In Genesis 22:12, the angel of the Lord said, "Do not lay a hand on the boy. . . . Do not do anything to him. Now I know that you fear God, because you have not withheld from me your son, your only son." God reaffirmed His everlasting covenant with Abraham because He knew that Abraham feared Him.

What changed in Abraham? He gained faith. Earlier he didn't trust God to protect his life. Later he was willing to sacrifice his hope of descendants, trusting that God would honor His promise to raise up a nation through Abraham's offspring.

Content

There are two broad categories of Old Testament people who had "fear of the Lord." The difference lies in how and why they feared Him. The first group feared the Lord in terror (see 1 Samuel 11:7; 2 Chronicles 14:14). They expected imminent destruction. They often hid in caves and holes to escape the day of the Lord and His terrible judgment (see Isaiah 2:10,17-21). In some translations the term *dread* captures this sense effectively.

The second group's fear was consistently associated with long life, knowledge, and wisdom (see Job 28:28; Psalm 19:9; Proverbs 1:7,29; 2:5). To fear God in this way is to rightly ascribe to Him all authority and power. Generally, those who reject God will eventually dread Him, while those who are His prudently fear Him.

So what about us? What tension should we feel between intimacy with our Father and awe before Him as the Creator of the universe? Exodus 20 provides an interesting insight. Immediately after receiving the Ten Commandments, the Israelites were terrified by the thunder, lightning, and smoke that signaled God's presence. In response, Moses told them, "Do not be afraid. God has come to test you, so that the fear of God will be with you to keep you from sinning" (verse 20).

God didn't come simply to terrify them. He wasn't trying to get an emotional response just to prove His power. But He did want the people to fear Him for their own sake. He wanted to give them a glimmer of the One with whom they had made promises of loyalty. God intended for this revelation of who He was to affect them so deeply that they would take His instructions seriously, even when disobedience felt better. Author and theologian Craig Blaising described the balance for all of God's children: "God has not come maliciously, but neither has He come permissively; and in between the two is grace."[1]

> *the fear of the Lord:* an inward attitude of humble reverence toward God, in light of His self-revelation, that results in outward expression of Christlikeness

According to this definition, the fear of the Lord involves two parts. The first is the inward attitude. This attitude is humble because as the Lord reveals His character, His majesty, His power and holiness, we are humbled before Him. We realize that God alone is worthy of our devotion and reverence (see Job 38–41; Psalm 33:8; Hebrews 12:28-29). The second part is the outward obedience, which flows from this inward humility. God reveals Himself to us so we will obey Him (see Deuteronomy 6:2-13). The two parts are linked.

As Christians, we express obedience by modeling our lives on Christ's. Christ Himself, the greatest revelation of God, is the best example of how we can live properly fearing Him (see Philippians 2:5-16).

How can we grow in our fear of the Lord? Here are three suggestions:

1. We can immerse ourselves in God's Word (see Psalm 119). The fear of the Lord grows with revelation of how magnificent He is. As we see His character and authority through the events and teaching of Scripture, our hearts will be drawn to have a proper reverence toward God.

2. We can ask the Lord regularly to unite our hearts to fear His name (see Psalm 86:11). God desires to reveal Himself to us and to align our heads and hearts to His character. This is a prayer He longs to answer.

3. We can live moment by moment in the reality of God's presence (see Psalm 139:7-12). When we forget about God in our daily schedule, we are not living in reality. We must cultivate a mindset that is ever aware of God's presence.

Conclusion

The fear of the Lord is the product of God's revelation. This knowledge leads to an attitude of humility and exhibits itself in obedience. When we truly fear the Lord, we have union between mind (what we think), heart (what we value and treasure), and body (what we do).

Assignment

Read *Session 8: Spirit*.

Complete *Biblical Exercise: John 15 and 16* beginning on page 55.

Spirit

In session 7, we discussed why a reverent perspective toward God is so important for our growth in holiness. This week we'll explore what it means to "walk by the Spirit" (Galatians 5:16, NASB). Our progress in integrity is directly related to the degree to which we learn to submit to and depend on the Holy Spirit.

Walking by the Spirit affects our ability to avoid the seven deadly sins. When we walk by the Spirit, we cannot simultaneously walk in sin. But walking by the Spirit leads to more than avoidance of sin; it leads to a godly life. In this session we will remember that in order to walk by the Spirit, we must see Him as a Person to whom we relate rather than as a lofty concept of goodness and power. In order to walk by the Spirit, we must orient our lives around Him.

Session Aims

Individual Aim: To explore what it means to walk by the Spirit in everyday life.

Group Aim: To discuss the challenges that each group member faces in walking by the Spirit and to gain insights from one another about how to rely on the Spirit more fully.

Preparation

Read *Session 8: Spirit.*

Complete *Biblical Exercise: John 15 and 16* beginning on page 55.

Introduction

In his article "Who's Afraid of the Holy Spirit?" Daniel Wallace tells a story that made him profoundly aware of his need for a vital relationship with the Spirit of God. Dr. Wallace is a highly respected professor in the New Testament department at Dallas Theological Seminary. His Greek grammar textbook is used worldwide. In 1992, Dr. Wallace's eight-year-old son, Andy, was diagnosed with renal cell carcinoma, a dangerous form of kidney cancer rarely found in children. In the midst of his pain and fear, Dr. Wallace sought solace in his faith, only to find that it had become what he calls "Christianity from the neck up." He writes,

> Through this experience I found that the Bible was not adequate. I needed God in a personal way—not as an object of my study, but as friend, guide, and comforter. I needed an existential experience of the Holy One. Quite frankly, I found that the Bible was not the answer. I found the Scriptures to be helpful—even authoritatively helpful—as a guide. But without my feeling God, the Bible gave me little solace. . . . I believe that I had depersonalized God so much that when I really needed him, I didn't know how to relate.[1]

Content

In describing his own experience, Dr. Wallace has identified a challenge that we all face. We easily allow God to become the subject of our study, a fascinating topic of theoretical investigation, but not the personal Lord to whom we are subject and on whom we are dependent. In the same way, we acquire head knowledge of the third person of the Trinity without experiencing heart connection with the Spirit who comforts us in our sorrow, guides us in our confusion, and enables us in our struggle against the flesh.

Learning to live the spiritual life requires that we move beyond a merely cerebral form of Christianity into a dynamic relationship with the Holy Spirit. Unfortunately for us, there is no simple formula for learning life in the Spirit. In our quest to become people of integrity, people whose lives are characterized by single-hearted devotion and fear of the Lord, we don't have a concrete set of instructions to follow. Rather, Paul gave us a simple admonition: "Walk by the Spirit."

Conclusion

In session 3, we examined how the flesh manifests itself in our lives. We saw that Paul identified an ongoing and ever-present struggle between the flesh and the Spirit. When he told the Galatians, "Walk by the Spirit, and you will not carry out the desire of the flesh" (Galatians 5:16, NASB), Paul indicated that these two are polar opposites.

If the life of the flesh is "the outlook oriented toward the self," then we can understand the life of the Spirit as "the outlook oriented toward the Spirit." If the life of the flesh is "that which pursues its own ends in self-sufficient inde- pendence of God,"[2] then the life of the Spirit is "that which pursues God's ends in complete dependence on the Spirit." Scot McKnight explains further:

> In general, we see something fundamentally important here as to how Paul depicts the Christian life. It is life in the Spirit, the life of a person who is surrendered to letting the Spirit have complete control. But we see here also that one does not gain this life by dis- cipline or by mustering up the energy. One does not huddle with oneself in the morning, gather together his or her forces, and charge onto the battlefield of life full of self-determined direction. Rather, the Christian life is a life of complete surrender to the Spirit.[3]

Biblical Exercise: John 15 and 16

Read John 15:1-17; 16:5-16. Also, review "A Method for the Biblical Exercises" beginning on page 15.

Observation — **"What Do I See?"**

1. Who are the persons (including God) in the passage? What is the con- dition of those persons?

2. What subjects did Jesus (as well as the author, John) discuss in the passage? What did Jesus and John assert?

3. Note the sequence in which Jesus made these assertions. (You might number them in order.)

4. What did Jesus emphasize? Are there repeated ideas and themes? How are the various parts related?

5. Why did Jesus say what He said? (How did He expect His audience to change after hearing it?)

Interpretation Phase 1—**"What Did It Mean Then?"**

1. Coming to Terms—Are there any words in the passage that you don't understand? Write down anything you found confusing about the passage.

2. Finding Where It Fits—What clues does the Bible give about the meaning of this passage?

   • Immediate Context (the passage being studied)

   • Remote Context (passages that come before and after the one being studied)

3. Getting into Their Sandals—An Exercise in Imagination

   • What are the main points of this passage? Summarize or write an outline of it.

- What do you think the apostles were supposed to take from this teaching of Christ? How did Jesus want this teaching to affect their thoughts and actions?

Interpretation Phase 2—"What Does It Mean Now?"

1. What is the timeless truth in the passage? In one or two sentences, write down what you learned about God from John 15 and 16.

2. How does that truth work today?

Application—"What Can I Do to Make This Truth Real?"

1. What can I do to make this truth real for myself?

2. For my family?

3. For my friends?

4. For the people who live near me?

5. For the rest of the world?

Assignment

Read *Session 9: Spiritual Disciplines.*

Complete the *Life Change: Spiritual Disciplines* exercise beginning on page 99.

Spiritual Disciplines

In session 8, we explored aspects of the Holy Spirit's role in the process of sanctification. We must never forget that sanctification is a process. One of the ways that we open ourselves to the Spirit's work is in exercising the spiritual disciplines. The spiritual disciplines are activities we do to practice dependence on Christ. They include studying the Bible, prayer, and others to be mentioned in this session.

However, they are means to an end. The Christian life is not a call to simply study the Bible and pray. The goal, as we discussed last session, is to grow in moment-by-moment dependence on God through the Spirit of God who indwells us. From the time God sent His Spirit to live with us, after Christ ascended to heaven, all believers have had the privilege of depending on the Spirit. He brings to mind revealed truth in our times of need and supports us in our pursuit of holiness. The spiritual disciplines, when we develop them into habits, help that process.

Session Aims

Individual Aim: To explore how to use spiritual disciplines while maintaining dependence on the Spirit.

Group Aim: To share ways the group can develop greater accountability in spiritual disciplines.

Preparation

Read *Session 9: Spiritual Disciplines.*

Complete the *Life Change: Spiritual Disciplines* exercise beginning on page 99.

Introduction

Jonathan Edwards was one of America's premier theologians and greatest preachers. Edwards lived by a list of resolutions. For example: "Resolved, never to do anything which I would be afraid to do if it were the last hour of my life."[1] This statement shows how serious he was about pursuing holiness. It reveals a man who understood the fear of the Lord and sought to live it.

Yet look at another of Edwards' resolutions: "Resolved, never to give over, nor in the least to slacken, my fight with my corruptions, however unsuccessful I may be."[2] What marvelous balance! Edwards resolved to fight the sin in his life but recognized that it would be a slow and painful process, one that would often feel unsuccessful. Defeat didn't weaken his resolve.

Content

Train yourself to be godly. (1 Timothy 4:7)

Pastor Donald Whitney describes spiritual disciplines like this:

> The spiritual disciplines are those personal and corporate disciplines that promote spiritual growth. They are habits of devotion and experiential Christianity that have been practiced by the people of God since biblical times.[3]

We need to develop habits of holiness while guarding ourselves from the dangers of both heartless discipline and slothfulness. The path of sanctification must avoid two pitfalls: legalism and passivity.

The terms *disciplines, exercises,* and *habits* make some of us fear that legalism will stifle our growth. R. Kent Hughes describes such sentiments: "For many, spiritual discipline means putting oneself back under the Law with a series of Draconian rules which no one can live up to—and which spawn frustration and spiritual death." Legalism reduces the sanctification process to a list of dos and don'ts and becomes an exercise in self-sufficiency. But there is a difference between legalism and disciplines, and this difference is in the motivation. As Hughes notes, "Legalism says, 'I will do this thing to gain merit with God,' while discipline says, 'I will do this because I love

God and want to please Him.'"[4] Our motives aren't always clear, even to us, but we can ask the Spirit to show us where we are practicing disciplines out of self-sufficiency rather than out of love for God.

The second pitfall to avoid is passivity. This is an attitude of "wait and see." To avoid any appearance of earning merit, this approach promotes "letting go" and "waiting for the Spirit to move" before taking any action. The motivation for this approach can be nothing more than personal laziness. This position sets up a false dichotomy between grace and action. As Dallas Willard notes, "Faith is not opposed to knowledge; it is opposed to sight. And grace is not opposed to effort; it is opposed to earning."[5] Richard Foster agrees and supports a more disciplined approach, calling it "the way of disciplined grace. It is 'grace' because it is free; it is 'disciplined' because there is something more for us to do."[6] Spiritual disciplines don't guarantee that we'll avoid the pitfalls of legalism or passivity, but they can serve as channels of grace.

Conclusion

For spiritual disciplines to help us grow, the Holy Spirit's work must accompany them. However, the Spirit can't force us to grow. We must be active in our dependent faith. Foster notes, "God has given us the disciplines of the spiritual life as a means of receiving His grace. The disciplines allow us to place ourselves before God so that He can transform us."[7]

Practicing the disciplines is like placing yourself in a channel for grace, with results similar to placing yourself in a channel for water. If you place yourself in a channel for water, you have a greater likelihood of getting wet. It's not a guarantee; sometimes the channel is dry and one must wait for the water. Likewise, sometimes the rains come and soak those who are not in the channel as much as those in it. But on the whole, those who are in the channel will regularly receive water.

As we practice the disciplines, we place ourselves in channels where God can pour out His grace into our lives. On the whole, those who make a commitment to pursue holiness through these channels of grace will find refreshment that only the Spirit can bring.

Paul tells us that self-control, or self-discipline, works hand in hand with the Holy Spirit. God gave us spirits of power, love, and self-control (see 2 Timothy 1:7). Self-control is a fruit of the Spirit (see Galatians 5:23).

Personal discipline and the Holy Spirit work together to produce fruit in our lives. So, just as we discipline ourselves to become godly, we must also always depend upon the Spirit to be fruitful. Therefore, we now turn our attention to the topic of the fruit of the Spirit.

Assignment

Read *Session 10: The Fruit of the Spirit.*

Complete the *Life Change: The Fruit of the Spirit* exercise beginning on page 101.

The Fruit of the Spirit

A plant can't produce fruit on its own. Plants need proper soil, moisture, and sunlight to mature to the point of producing fruit. If those elements are present, the plant will naturally produce fruit. Yet the fact that the fruit is born naturally doesn't diminish the reality that work has to happen in the plant for the fruit to be produced. The work of that plant is consistent with the nature of the plant, so it's natural, but it's still work.

As we saw in session 9, we have a responsibility to actively depend on Christ. In this session, we will observe what happens when we inwardly depend on the Spirit.

Session Aims

Individual Aim: To consider how you have seen the fruit of the Spirit in the lives of other group members.

Group Aim: To identify the fruit of the Spirit in each other's lives, examining the obstacles to fruitfulness and the ways group members might overcome them.

Preparation

Read *Session 10: The Fruit of the Spirit*.

Complete the *Life Change: The Fruit of the Spirit* exercise beginning on page 101.

Introduction

Just as we had to have an active faith in receiving Christ, we pursue holiness in Christ actively. Our faith in Christ for salvation was active in the sense that we had to respond, even though it was not active in the sense of any of our good works winning us merit for salvation.

In His conversation with Nicodemus, Jesus said rebirth requires believing in Him (see John 3:16-18). Salvation is not granted in the context of passivity. Though the power for salvation is not our own, we are responsible to act. The action that ought to follow salvation is a movement of the heart toward dependence on God, or what is called "walking in the Spirit." James tells us that walking in faith results in good works, the outward expression of dependence on God's power (see James 2:14-26). God wants us to produce outward good deeds "so that it may be seen plainly that what he has done has been done through God" (John 3:21).

Content

Scripture is filled with images taken from the world of horticulture. For example, the Old Testament repeatedly uses the images of an olive tree and a vineyard to refer to Israel (see Psalm 52:8; Isaiah 3:14; Jeremiah 11:16; Ezekiel 19:10-12). Christ refers to Himself as "the vine" and His followers as "branches," promising that those who abide in Him will "bear much fruit" (John 15:5). And Paul talked about the kind of fruit that would characterize those who "walk in the Spirit" when he identified the "fruit of the Spirit" as "love, joy, peace, patience, kindness, goodness, faithfulness, gentleness, and self-control" (Galatians 5:22-23).

About this ninefold fruit, Philip Kenneson writes,

> These metaphors and images underscore the importance in the Christian life of both work and grace. All farmers know that there is always more work to be done than there is time to do it; nevertheless, these same farmers also understand that much of what happens to the crops is beyond their control. There is much for the farmer to do, but the farmer cannot make the seed sprout, the sun shine or the rain fall. In fact, it is only because the farmer trusts that these good gifts will continue to be given that the challenging and risk-filled enterprise of farming is undertaken at all. Grace and effort, gift and work: these must be held together. Unfortunately, Christians often either pit these against each other or emphasize one to the exclusion of the other. The wisdom of the farmer reminds us that both are required, in full measure, in order to grow anything worth harvesting. The same holds for the life of the Spirit. There is always plenty of work to be done, but no one who

undertakes that work should do so without realizing that growth in the Spirit is first of all the gift of God.[1]

We must keep this understanding in mind as we explore the Spirit's fruit. Only the Spirit can enable us to bear fruit, but our contribution to cultivating the fruit is essential too.

Conclusion

Growing fruit takes time, and the fruit of the Spirit grows particularly slowly. Sometimes the growth is imperceptible, but the Spirit's presence in our lives guarantees that growth will occur. Our commitment to growth wanes easily when we grow tired of waiting, but we must not become discouraged. Rather, we must continue to do our part by laying aside our preoccupation with ourselves and focusing on others—both God and our neighbors. As we learn to do this, we will see fruit grow that only the Spirit of God working within us can produce.

Assignment

Read *Session 11: Growing in Integrity.*

Growing in Integrity

In this session, we will take time for some concluding thoughts about integrity. How does a person grow in integrity over a lifetime? Each season of life brings new circumstances and challenges to our growth in integrity.

Session Aims

Individual Aim: To consider how you will pursue growth in integrity throughout all the seasons of your life.

Group Aim: To challenge and sharpen one another to pursue a lifetime of growth in integrity.

Preparation

Read *Session 11: Growing in Integrity.*

Introduction

To grow in integrity over a lifetime, we need to cultivate certain disciplines. For example, we must have consistent exposure to God's Word through personal study and listening to preaching. We need to worship corporately and pray. But is competency in a variety of spiritual disciplines sufficient? Is the Christian life like a spiritual checklist: "I've learned how to share my faith, how to study my Bible, and how to be selfless in my relationship with my spouse"? What happens to our competencies in all these areas when we face new challenges? What happens to our morning prayer time when we have an infant who wakes at 5 AM every morning? How do we learn to love a new coworker who seems to be so different from the person he or she replaced? How do we adjust to these new circumstances?

Content

As we discussed in our session on the Spirit, many Christians want to make the spiritual life a simple, step-by-step process. We live in a culture obsessed with quick fixes and instant gratification, and this obsession can easily affect the way we approach the spiritual life. But when we reflect on our growth in the Christian life, we recognize that growth in integrity rarely comes quickly or painlessly. Rather, God works in us over extended periods of time and through diverse circumstances. Each season provides new challenges and new resources for growth in integrity. How would you describe the season of life you are in right now? What unique opportunities for growth does this season provide?

Consider, for example, the apostle Paul's experience in learning contentment. He claimed he had learned to be content "in any and every situation" (Philippians 4:11-12). In order to fully develop contentment, he had to learn how to be content in seasons when he had plenty as well as in seasons when he had little. Each of these seasons provided unique challenges and unique opportunities for growth.

In a time of want we may struggle with the temptation to envy others who are better off materially. Wanting more may be a basic desire to have adequate food, shelter, and coverings, or it could be the desire to change our social status. In a season of poverty we face a unique challenge for contentment.

In contrast, material excess presents us with a different challenge to contentment. We may be tempted to exceed the material success of others for the social distinction it can provide. Or we may become obsessed with seeking more material wealth in order to attain financial security for the future. In either case, we might lose a sense of contentment.

Though it may be possible for us to learn the virtue of contentment through experience in only one season of life, such as in a state of poverty, it develops more fully when learned in a variety of circumstances. When we apply this principle to the whole of our pursuit of biblical integrity, we realize that God constantly uses new life circumstances to develop in us a more complete image of Christ. In the many seasons of life, we will inevitably see times when we struggle in some area of our faith, even an area that we had previously considered a strength. This often occurs when we face an entirely new set of circumstances.

For instance, dealing with failure requires a consistent experience of God's forgiveness and the perseverance to press on. Obviously, failure is not God's desire for us, but He uses new circumstances, including failure, to develop our godly character.

That's what happened to the apostle Peter. He experienced special revelation after Christ's ascension that convinced him to take the gospel to the Gentiles (see Acts 10). He clearly understood that no dividing wall should stand between believing Jews and Gentiles. He even responded to the revelation by welcoming Gentiles into the young church (see Acts 11:1-18). However, when Peter was later in Antioch with Paul and Barnabas, he failed to live what he had learned. Some other Jewish believers came to town from Jerusalem, and Peter withdrew from Gentile believers in order to avoid offending these visitors (see Galatians 2:11-14).

Paul had to confront Peter. Peter had failed when he faced a new set of circumstances with a new form of temptation. Even though Peter had learned the principle that Jew and Gentile are one in Christ, he chose to live contrary to that principle when put under pressure. We cannot know from the text (Galatians 2) exactly what his reasoning was at that time, but he needed a brother to confront him, a fresh experience of the forgiveness of God, and an attitude of diligence to press on in his Christian walk.

God has us on a journey to transform our entire lives from how we are at our initial salvation to a life marked by Christian maturity. If we expect to learn to live out godly character the way we learn concepts in a book, we foolishly ignore the crucial truth that the fruit of the Spirit must develop over time amidst various life circumstances. By His grace, God works in us throughout the seasons of our lives, in successes and failures, teaching us crucial lessons about ourselves and about Himself, conforming us to the image of His Son.

Conclusion

Throughout our lives, we must (1) remain alert to the temptations that play into our weaknesses, (2) experience grace in Christ when we fail, and (3) maintain the attitude of a diligent learner, so that the Lord may continue to mold us into His image for the rest of our lives.

Life Change

Introduction

"Life Change" will lead you into a challenging examination of sin and righteousness. You will struggle with sin throughout your life. Your identity in Christ beckons you to a life of holiness, but your heritage as a sinner living independently of God continues to influence your attitudes and actions. "Life Change" addresses both resisting sin and pursuing growth in holiness.

"Life Change" starts with an inventory of your personal values. What you truly value in any given circumstance determines your attitude and actions. The tool examines seven broad categories of sin, called the seven deadly sins. These categories describe tendencies in which personal values conflict with biblical principles and God's will. Each person has unique tendencies to sin. Identifying your personal tendencies to sin will help you resist those tendencies. Confessing sin keeps personal sin tendencies from remaining hidden and therefore opens up opportunities for gaining support to resist sin. The exercise called "A Letter from Your Tempter" provides a creative way for you to confess areas of sin to others.

The second part of the "Life Change" tool turns to positive growth. Exercising a spiritual discipline will enable you to experience dependence on God in a new way. Examining the fruit of the Spirit will encourage you to see how God has already been transforming you and to set your sights on new areas for growth.

Though "Life Change" may be used profitably by individuals, it has been designed to be done in a small group. This process can solidify the sense of community you experience with a group that has been together for a short time, or it can deepen that sense with a group that has been together longer. Given the sensitive nature of the content that people will be exploring in these exercises, care should be taken when the content is shared with a group. Coed groups may want to consider splitting up times into single-sex groups for sharing times. Some of the content from the "Life Change" exercises may need to be adjusted for sharing in a group setting.

You will do the "Life Change" exercises in private. Each exercise provides instructions. You will get out of the exercises what you put into them in terms of time and focused attention. May this process be a significant time for you to increase your understanding of your growth in righteousness!

Belief and Practice

In this exercise, you will identify several biblical beliefs that you have learned to practice in some area of your life. You might not practice a belief perfectly, and you might not practice it in every area of your life. Nonetheless, it is an area in which you have experienced significant growth.

For instance, maybe your faith has helped you lessen your anxiety about work deadlines. Or perhaps God has convicted you and helped you change from having a cynical demeanor to one of encouragement when you relate to your relatives.

The following pages contain a list of biblical principles that may help you identify areas of past growth. It is not an exclusive list, so feel free to choose other biblical principles that apply to your own experience. Choose up to three biblical principles that you have come to believe *and* practice. Record them on page 80, and in the appropriate space, describe the process by which you grew to practice that belief. Consider the influence that Scripture, prayer, and other believers played in your life-change experience.

Biblical Principles

Liberality

> *Give to the one who asks you, and do not turn away from the one who wants to borrow from you. (Matthew 5:42)*

Mercy

> *Love your enemies and pray for those who persecute you. (Matthew 5:44)*

Simplicity

Do not store up for yourselves treasures on earth, where moth and rust destroy, and where thieves break in and steal. (Matthew 6:19)

Contentment

Do not worry about your life, what you will eat or drink; or about your body, what you will wear. (Matthew 6:25)

Hope

Therefore we do not lose heart. Though outwardly we are wasting away, yet inwardly we are being renewed day by day. For our light and momentary troubles are achieving for us an eternal glory that far outweighs them all. So we fix our eyes not on what is seen, but on what is unseen. For what is seen is temporary, but what is unseen is eternal. (2 Corinthians 4:16-18)

Christian Fellowship

Do not be yoked together with unbelievers. For what do righteousness and wickedness have in common? Or what fellowship can light have with darkness? (2 Corinthians 6:14)

Faith

But by faith we eagerly await through the Spirit the righteousness for which we hope. For in Christ Jesus neither circumcision nor uncircumcision has any value. The only thing that counts is faith expressing itself through love. (Galatians 5:5-6)

Temperance

Having lost all sensitivity, they have given themselves over to sensuality so as to indulge in every kind of impurity, with a continual lust for more. . . . You were taught, with regard to your former way of life, to put off your old self, which is being corrupted by its deceitful desires; to be made new in the attitude of your minds; and to put on the new self, created to be like God in true righteousness and holiness. (Ephesians 4:19,22-24)

Edification

Do not let any unwholesome talk come out of your mouths, but only what is helpful for building others up according to their needs, that it may benefit those who listen. (Ephesians 4:29)

Humility

Do nothing out of selfish ambition or vain conceit, but in humility consider others better than yourselves. (Philippians 2:3)

Perseverance

Brothers, I do not consider myself yet to have taken hold of it. But one thing I do: Forgetting what is behind and straining toward what is ahead, I press on toward the goal to win the prize for which God has called me heavenward in Christ Jesus. (Philippians 3:13-14)

Praise

Rejoice in the Lord always. I will say it again: Rejoice! (Philippians 4:4)

Prayer

Do not be anxious about anything, but in everything, by prayer and petition, with thanksgiving, present your requests to God. (Philippians 4:6)

Contemplation and Reflection

Set your minds on things above, not on earthly things. For you died, and your life is now hidden with Christ in God. (Colossians 3:2-3)

Forbearance

Therefore, as God's chosen people, holy and dearly loved, clothe yourselves with compassion, kindness, humility, gentleness and patience. Bear with each other and forgive whatever grievances you may have against one another. (Colossians 3:12-13)

Industriousness

If a man will not work, he shall not eat. (2 Thessalonians 3:10)

Purity of Speech/Doctrine

Avoid godless chatter, because those who indulge in it will become more and more ungodly. Their teaching will spread like gangrene. (2 Timothy 2:16-17)

Hospitality

Do not forget to entertain strangers, for by so doing some people have entertained angels without knowing it. (Hebrews 13:2)

Fidelity

Marriage should be honored by all, and the marriage bed kept pure. (Hebrews 13:4)

Confession

Confess your sins to each other. (James 5:16)

Sympathy

Live in harmony with one another; be sympathetic, love as brothers, be compassionate and humble. (1 Peter 3:8)

Evangelism

Always be prepared to give an answer to everyone who asks you to give the reason for the hope that you have. (1 Peter 3:15)

Loyalty

Above all, love each other deeply, because love covers over a multitude of sins. (1 Peter 4:8)

Generosity

If anyone has material possessions and sees his brother in need but has no pity on him, how can the love of God be in him? (1 John 3:17)

Love

God is love. Whoever lives in love lives in God, and God in him. In this way, love is made complete among us so that we will have confidence on the day of judgment, because in this world we are like him. There is no fear in love. But perfect love drives out fear, because fear has to do with punishment. The one who fears is not made perfect in love. We love because he first loved us. (1 John 4:16-19)

Principle #1 _____

Practice:

Principle #2 _____

Practice:

Principle #3 _____

Practice:

Spiritual Discipline Exercise — Thanksgiving

Now that you have spent some time considering how God has been transforming your life, take time to offer thanks to Him. You may decide to take a half hour one morning this week to pray or journal, listing all that you are thankful for. Or spend a few minutes every day, perhaps before bed or after you wake up, and thank Him. One thing to thank Him for is His commitment to transforming you to be more like Christ.

Seven Deadly Sins

Slowly read the definitions of each category of sin and the descriptions of how each manifests itself in a person's life. As you read, underline any phrases, lines, or sections that describe your behavior. Be honest.

After you have worked through all seven, take time to review what you underlined. There may be many areas of sin that God wants to address in your entire life. The key now is letting Him reveal what He wants you to address right now. However, we are often blind to our own sin. The Spirit may bring to mind some areas of sin, or He may use recent interactions with others to point out areas to you.

Identify one or two of the seven that you would say are the predominant sin categories you are currently struggling with. Make notes for yourself describing the personal dynamics of those particular areas of sin. For example, if you struggle with greed, the personal dynamic may be as follows: "When I'm around my old college buddies and see the cars they drive and the homes they live in, I find myself obsessed with having those nice things too. I don't desire to have more than they have or to be better than they are. I particularly want to enjoy the luxuries of a car and a house like theirs."

You may want to include in your notes descriptions of those sins from various angles in your life. For instance, how does the struggle with greed show up at work? With friends? With family?

Be prepared to share with the group the areas of sin with which you struggle. You won't have to go into detail about the dynamics of those areas of sin at this point, only the category (envy, greed, and so on). Also, if you are in a coed group, you will probably separate into single-sex groups for this discussion.

Envy

Envy is being dissatisfied with our lives, talents, and gifts and focusing on the circumstances of another's life. It begrudges someone their status, material possessions, or the relationships and good will that they have earned from others in the community.

—Kaye Briscoe King[1]

When the men were returning home after David had killed the Philistine, the women came out from all the towns of Israel to meet King Saul with singing and dancing, with joyful songs and with tambourines and lutes. As they danced, they sang:

> *"Saul has slain his thousands,*
> *and David his tens of thousands."*

Saul was very angry; this refrain galled him. "They have credited David with tens of thousands," he thought, "but me with only thousands. What more can he get but the kingdom?" And from that time on Saul kept a jealous eye on David. (1 Samuel 18:6-9)

With respect to envy, many of them are wont to experience movements of displeasure at the spiritual good of others, which cause them a certain sensible grief at being outstripped upon this road, so that they would prefer not to hear others praised; for they become displeased at others' virtues and sometimes they cannot refrain from contradicting what is said in praise of them, depreciating it as far as they can; and their annoyance thereat grows because the same is not said of them, for they would fain be preferred in everything. All this is clean contrary to charity, which, as Saint Paul says, rejoices in goodness.

—St. John of the Cross, *Dark Night of the Soul*, VII

Manifestations:

Actively trying to dissuade others from admiring or accepting anyone we envy. Setting up an unfair rivalry or competition with that person. Being happy and satisfied when bad fortune befalls another. Belittling and planting seeds of doubt about another's character. Gossiping. Devising ways of destroying someone, sometimes with a long-range plan. Being dissatisfied with our physical, emotional, intellectual, and spiritual selves. Being unwilling to be content with our station or lot in life. A person can become our flash point for an obsession. We encourage criticism and antagonism against the person through sarcasm, teasing, or cutting him down. Envy can be masked as contempt for a person's culture, position, and talents or for someone who is in authority over us.

—Kaye Briscoe King

Greed

Greed is a desire for inordinate amounts of personal possessions or status. Greed uses others for our personal gain in spite of any harm that this manipulation may cause them.

—Kaye Briscoe King

Keep your lives free from the love of money and be content with what you have, because God has said,

> Godliness with contentment is great gain. For we brought nothing into the world, and we can take nothing out of it. But if we have food and clothing, we will be content with that. People who want to get rich fall into temptation and a trap and into many foolish and harmful desires that plunge men into ruin and destruction. For the love of money is a root of all kinds of evil. Some people, eager for money, have wandered from the faith and pierced themselves with many griefs. (1 Timothy 6:6-10)

> "Never will I leave you;
> never will I forsake you." (Hebrews 13:5)

This is greed: living to possess anything—stamps, dolls, autographed balls, books, CDs, paintings, figurines, toys, property, cars, contacts/acquaintances, whatever—with the primary objective of owning, the preoccupation with having, the obsession of getting, and/or the dedication of too much of our lives or the investment of too much of our hearts.

—Dr. William Backus[2]

Now you can see, my son, how brief's the sport
of all those goods that are in Fortune's care,
for which the tribe of men contend and brawl;
for all the gold that is or ever was
beneath the moon could never offer rest
to even one of these exhausted spirits.

Dante Alighieri, The Divine Comedy, Inferno, Canto VII

Manifestations:

Putting possessions in place of God. Being ambitious and disdaining morality, the law, or the rights of others. Pursuing status, material possessions, reputation, or power. Believing that all's fair in competition and, thus, becoming ruthless and unjust. Being too possessive or protective of our children, spouse, or friends. Being self-centered. Refusing to set boundaries. Avoiding conflict by not correcting or disciplining children for fear they will not love us. Deliberately engaging others in illegal or unethical activities. Manipulating others . . . to do our will through threat of physical violence, withdrawal of affection, cajoling, or whining. Letting control and power be motivating forces in our lives. Being too eager to give advice or possess authority. Attempting to have others in debt to us so we can exert power. Using flattery, gifts, favoritism, or even covert bribery to win support, affection, or authority.

Backing down from personal standards or refusing to be involved with or defend people of lesser means or position; fearing being stigmatized by leaders or the wealthy. Being dishonest by stealing or fencing stolen goods, cheating on exams, falsifying records, or evading taxes. Being narcissistic. Believing we are entitled to something because of who we are. Wasting possessions, talent, or natural resources. Living beyond our income in order to impress others or sustain our present standard of living. Embezzling. Gambling in such a way that gambling controls us. Intriguing or conspiring. Borrowing, sponging, weaseling, or playing on the good will of others in order not to use our own money, time, or talent. Being stingy or being indifferent to the homeless and hungry. Failing to engage in teamwork in our workplace or at home.

—Kaye Briscoe King

Lust

We lust when we seek another god or material satisfaction to fill the emptiness in our lives. Lust is an excessive, driving desire for personal sexual gratification, disregarding God's intended purpose for sexuality, in order to fulfill our own inordinate needs.

—Kaye Briscoe King

"You have heard that it was said, 'Do not commit adultery.' But I tell you that anyone who looks at a woman lustfully has already committed adultery with her in his heart." (Matthew 5:27-28)

Lust is often defined as the desire for inappropriate physical intimacy with a person, or the image of a person (such as computer-generated images), other than a spouse. It is a sin that many people must guard against throughout their entire lives.

However, within marriage, there is an additional element of lust that is often overlooked. When a husband feels lonely and demands that his wife engage sexually with him to fulfill his desire for intimacy, he is sinning. In Ephesians, Paul lifted the bar for marriage higher than it has ever been before or since. He said a husband ought to tenderly care for his wife's best interest, not primarily with a view to his own desires:

In this same way, husbands ought to love their wives as their own bodies. He who loves his wife loves himself. After all, no one ever hated his own body, but he feeds and cares for it, just as Christ does the church. (Ephesians 5:28-29)

Sexual intimacy can become the focal point of marriage, even for the believer. If a husband uses manipulation to persuade his wife to enter into sexual activity with him, he may be lusting after his wife. For instance, a husband comes home after work loaded with flowers and eager to help cook dinner, wash the dishes, and clean up the house. Then he initiates physical intimacy with his wife, and she asks to postpone it until tomorrow. The husband suddenly changes demeanor and becomes very short with her. He withdraws from her and goes to bed without a word. Could it be that he wanted only her body? Was he lusting after her physically while not truly caring for her interests before his own? Did his longing for physical intimacy interfere with his ability to see what would be loving for her?

In other words, lust may include an inappropriate pursuit of your spouse. If we are consumed with a pursuit of sexual intimacy beyond its proper role as an expression of love between husband and wife, we are struggling with lust.

Hostility toward sex also falls under the category of lust, as the following manifestations describe. It is no more godly to be obsessed against sex than for it.

Manifestations:

Misusing sex for personal gratification. Violating the church's marriage laws, such as those concerning adultery. Lack of consideration for one's partner in the marital relationship. Indulging sexually outside marriage in thought, word, or deed, alone or with others. Acting or fantasizing that leads to sexual perversion or addiction. Frequenting adult movie houses or reading sexual magazines. Engaging in voyeurism or indecent exposure. Molesting children. Raping. Engaging in prostitution or other promiscuous activities. Sodomizing. Stimulating sexual desires in others. Being immodest with intent to seduce. Condemning sex as evil in itself. Repressing sex. Refusing to seek help or adequate instruction for problems concerning sex. Prudery. Deliberately inflicting pain (whether mental, sexual, or emotional) on others. Tormenting animals. Holding someone against his or her will. Teasing. Denying that one's own sexuality is a gift from God. Being unwilling to inform our own children about sex.

—Kaye Briscoe King

Sloth

Sloth is the act of refusing to use our natural gifts and talents for emotional and spiritual growth. It is laziness or an unwillingness to perform our duties, work, and studies or pay attention to our needs and those of others.

—Kaye Briscoe King

For even when we were with you, we gave you this rule: "If a man will not work, he shall not eat."

We hear that some among you are idle. They are not busy; they are busybodies. Such people we command and urge in the Lord Jesus Christ to settle down and earn the bread they eat. And as for you, brothers, never tire of doing what is right. (2 Thessalonians 3:10-13)

If once they failed to find in prayer the satisfaction which their taste required . . . they would prefer not to return to it: sometimes they leave it; at other times they continue it unwillingly. . . . These persons likewise find it irksome when they are commanded to do that wherein they take no pleasure. Because they aim at spiritual sweetness and consolation, they are too weak to have the fortitude and bear the trials of perfection. They resemble those who are softly nurtured and who run fretfully away from everything that is hard, and take offense at the Cross, wherein consist the delights of the spirit.

—St. John of the Cross, *Dark Night of the Soul*, VII

Fulfilling our responsibilities requires some effort on our part. God designed human beings to work. Even in Eden, Adam was given responsibility: "Be fruitful and increase in number; fill the earth and subdue it. Rule over the fish of the sea and the birds of the air and over every creature that moves on the ground" (Genesis 1:28). Human beings have labor as a fundamental, divinely mandated purpose.

Spiritual growth also requires effort. If people desire to experience the abundant Christian life while remaining idle in their faith, they will be disappointed. Consider Paul's example of exertion:

I press on to take hold of that for which Christ Jesus took hold of me. Brothers, I do not consider myself yet to have taken hold of it. But one thing I do: Forgetting what is behind and straining toward what is ahead, I press on toward the goal to win the prize for which God has called me heavenward in Christ Jesus. (Philippians 3:12-14)

Manifestations:

Neglecting our family, such as being unwilling to follow through on relationships, courtesies, and concern for family members. Avoiding working through conflict. Procrastinating when we do not find immediate payoffs. Living in a dream world. Avoiding social obligations or becoming busy with irrelevant tasks in order to avoid important commitments. Spending an inordinate amount of time on rest, recreation, television, reading, etc. Always looking for easy answers and shortcuts to solutions. Putting pleasure above all else. Not assuming responsibility for our work by wasting time, . . . producing inadequate work, not meeting deadlines, or leaving our tasks for others to complete. Avoiding spiritual growth. Ignoring the needs and concerns of our employees. Not treating people of lesser means with dignity and being unwilling to go out of our way to accommodate those in need. Lacking concern for injustice done to others. Being unwilling to undergo hardships without complaining. . . . Failing to fulfill spiritual and religious obligations, such as attending church regularly.

—Kaye Briscoe King

Gluttony

Gluttony seeks happiness, pleasure, and security in the obsessive use of drink, drugs, sex, smoking, work, or any activity that is harmful to ourselves or others.

—Kaye Briscoe King

While you may not find yourself craving food compulsively, gluttony may still be a concern. Gluttony is often associated with food, but basically it is a pursuit of pleasure. Whereas lust is concerned more with intimacy and the satisfaction that comes with feeling connected with another person, gluttony pursues physical pleasure for its own sake. Gluttony involves an addiction to a physical pleasure.

Consider the saying "Some eat to live, I live to eat." You may put in the place of eating any activity of physical pleasure: "Some men enjoy sexuality with their wives as a natural part of their relational intimacy; I am obsessed with my wife as an object of pleasure." Any number of things that result in physical pleasure can be the object of a glutton's desire. It is quite possible that both a lust for intimacy and a gluttonous desire to experience sexual pleasure are involved.

Addiction to one object of physical pleasure might not be the only expression of gluttony. Shrewd gluttons realize what Søren Kierkegaard wrote about in *Either/Or*.[3] Kierkegaard explained that physical pleasure reaches its pinnacle if the person diversifies the experience of pleasure from various objects. If the glutton pursues pleasure in moderation from various objects, he will more fully experience the pleasure from each source. So gluttony can be hidden by the diversity of pleasure sought. For example, you get a massage, go out for a good meal, and retreat home for sex with your spouse. Having all of these experiences in a given day is not in itself sinful. However, if you rely on these diverse objects of pleasure to escape the struggles of life, you are misguided. One way to test your heart is to determine how you might feel if these pleasures were removed from your life. Would you demand from God that He return your meat entrees, or would you be content with bread and potatoes?

Manifestations:

Being self-indulgent in any pleasure—such as food, drink, drugs, or sex—that may lead to an addiction or, at the minimum, interfere with our social or vocational abilities. Being a perfectionist or demanding unrealistically high standards. Exaggerating our self-importance or being preoccupied with fantasies involving power, wealth, and reputation. Acting as if we are superior to others. Neglecting our health through lack of rest, recreation, exercise, wholesome diet, or balanced lifestyle. Refusing to care for our teeth. Refusing to seek counseling and face our participation in the addictive or dependency processes. Manipulating in order to sustain our addiction.

Becoming rigid and intolerant. Condemning others' pleasures as evil to squelch our own attachment to pleasure. Being a religious fanatic about sex in order to help ourselves detach from an inactive addiction that we have just under the surface. Denying the seriousness of our attachments and how the object of these affections consumes a great deal of our time. Substituting addictions for reality in order to block out pain, suffering, and our circumstances. Allowing them to become our false gods while turning our back on God. Being unwilling to accept help because of our love and loyalty to our attachment. Neglecting our spiritual walk. Having a tendency to become manic and unrealistic. Lacking self-discipline. Looking for a shortcut to success in order to get something for nothing. Having an over-attachment to grief because of past failures and feelings of unworthiness. Refusing to use things of the world in a balanced way.

Gluttony changes into an addiction when the attachment and any ensuing illnesses become a means of escape from intimacy and the responsibilities of our relationships with God, self, and others.

—Kaye Briscoe King

Pride

Pride occurs when we push God aside, become the center of our own universe, and act as if the world revolves around us and is under our control. It is a rebellion against God's sovereignty.

—Kaye Briscoe King

Fools say to themselves, "There is no God." (Psalm 14:1, NET)

As these [young Christians] feel themselves to be very fervent and diligent in spiritual things and devout exercises, from this prosperity . . . there often comes to them, through their imperfections, a certain kind of secret pride, whence they come to have some degree of satisfaction with their works and with themselves. And hence there comes to them likewise a certain desire, which is somewhat vain, and at times very vain, to speak of spiritual things in the presence of others, and sometimes even to teach such things rather than to learn them. They condemn others in their heart when they see that they have not the kind of devotion which they themselves desire; and sometimes they even say this in words, herein resembling the Pharisee, who boasted of himself, praising God for his own good works and despising the publican.

—St. John of the Cross, *Dark Night of the Soul*, II

Pride at its essence is an attitude that denies the existence of God. It is an attempt to exert oneself as an independent being. However, when we foster such an attitude, we are merely deceiving ourselves. In a culture where independence is so highly valued, pride is often hard to notice. We fail to realize that any movement we make with an independent attitude is rooted in pride.

When we think that we can, through will alone, accomplish a goal, we are deceived. Even "Christian" behavior can be done pridefully, in independence. If we try to live up to some status quo of behavior in our church community on our own power and merit, we are deceived. We are ignoring the reality that the Almighty gives us life and breath.

Besides being dependent upon God's sovereignty, we are also dependent on other people. We are not individual islands. To say to oneself, *It's just me and God*, is a form of pride. To be Christian is to be part of the body of Christ. We must not think we can live the Christian life as God intended in isolation from other Christians. We need others to sustain us.

Manifestations:

Depending on ourselves rather than on God. Expecting others to treat us as if we are a god. Being self-absorbed and leaving no time for God. Refusing to love and trust God; refusing to accept forgiveness from others, ourselves, or God, because we judge ourselves as not perfect (as we should be, since we are taking God's place). Pitying ourselves because we think our sins make us less respectable.

Attempting to control or predict the future by using spiritualism, astrology, fortune-telling, black magic, or superstition. Not practicing gratitude for others' gifts, knowledge, or good works.

Being territorial about our status. Acting as if we were better, further advanced, or more virtuous. Practicing hypocrisy (judging others harshly for faults that we ourselves possess). Refusing to recognize our own sins because to admit wrong or lack of perfection reveals that we are less than we think we are. Discounting our sins by minimizing or rationalizing: "Boys will be boys," or "That is just natural for women to do," or "That is the way teens normally act." Being too sensitive and refusing to see that we can grow from constructive criticism. Refusing to receive guidance from our community.

Refusing to take responsibility for . . . what we have done. Being unwilling to make amends and restitution. Lying or deceiving to escape discipline. Letting someone else take the blame because he is dispensable and we are not. . . . Exaggerating, interrupting, talking too much or in hyperbole. Taking center stage in an attempt to claim wisdom or abilities that we do not possess. Behaving ostentatiously in order to focus attention on ourselves. Having inordinate shyness because we feel we are not perfect. Being performance driven. Refusing to admit wrong or apologize in order to save face and avoid damage to our status in the community.

Refusing to accept less than excellence in food, drink, lodging, or another's performance. Being aggravated by the irritating habits of others. Being a bigot and saying our customs, race, religion, dress, and culture are superior to those of others. Overspending time and money on how we present ourselves, our home, or office in order to impress others. Showing superiority by thinking that we should not have to do what others do, such as work, chores, etc. Taking credit for our abilities and accomplishments rather than giving God or others credit for thoughts, insights, etc. Having to be the only one who has a credible idea or plan. Reinforcing our superiority by being overbearing, argumentative, and opinionated. Being legends in our own minds.

—Kaye Briscoe King

Anger

Anger becomes a sin when it takes the form of rebellion, revenge, or retaliation; causes harm to self or others; or sets an obstacle in the way of our relationship with God.

—Kaye Briscoe King

When their delight and pleasure in spiritual things come to an end, they naturally become embittered, and bear that lack of sweetness which they have to suffer with a bad grace, which affects all that they do; and they very easily become irritated over the smallest matter—sometimes, indeed, none can tolerate them. . . .

There are other of these spiritual persons, again, who fall into another kind of spiritual wrath: this happens when they become irritated at the sins of others, and keep watch on those others with a sort of uneasy zeal. At times the impulse comes to them to reprove them angrily . . . and set themselves up as masters of virtue. . . .

There are others who are vexed with themselves when they observe their own imperfectness, and display an impatience that is not humility; so impatient are they about this that they would fain be saints in a day. Many of these persons purpose to accomplish a great deal and make grand resolutions; yet, as they are not humble and have no misgivings about themselves, the more resolutions they make, the greater is their fall and the greater their annoyance, since they have not the patience to wait for that which God will give them when it pleases Him.

—St. John of the Cross, *Dark Night of the Soul*, V

But no man can tame the tongue. It is a restless evil, full of deadly poison. With the tongue we praise our Lord and Father, and with it we curse men, who have been made in God's likeness. Out of the same mouth come praise and cursing. My brothers, this should not be. (James 3:8-10)

One of the most common ways anger tempts the believer is with the simple phrase "I'm right." The issue is not always who is logically correct. The person who struggles with anger may well be "right" most of the time. However, we shouldn't impose our judgments in any manner we choose, even if our judgments are correct (and often they aren't). We are called to love, not to be "right." Sometimes loving others involves communicating what is right and what is not, but that communication shouldn't be guided by a passion-filled anger.

Manifestations:

Hating God. Refusing to allow Him into our lives. Turning our backs on a personal relationship with Him. Refusing to use our talents and gifts or pursue the mission God has given us. Blaming others (God, parents, spouse) and not accepting responsibility for the negative conditions we have brought on ourselves and the inner decisions we have made that have contributed to our unhappiness.

Being cynical. Purposely trying to ruin someone's reputation. Gossiping. Using profanity, grumbling, or attacking someone verbally (such as quarreling, nagging, rudeness, or raging) or physically (such as hitting, torture, or murder). Harsh or excessive punishment of children or others over whom we have authority. Forcing our will on others. Seeking revenge and retaliation.

Turning our anger against ourselves, such as through self-mutilation, overeating, bulimia, anorexia, or pushing ourselves to overwork or be perfect. . . . Refusing to let anger emerge and thus causing depression. Allowing anger to manifest itself in disease and conditions harmful to the body. Self-pity.

Anger is out of order when we refuse to forgive and are unwilling to let go of bitterness or love another as God does. We refuse to love the unlovable or our enemies. Anger in the form of passive-aggressive behavior is demonstrated when we ostracize another person, spoil another's pleasure (by snubbing or being moody or uncooperative), or physically or emotionally sabotage someone.

—Kaye Briscoe King

Spiritual Discipline Exercise — Silence and Solitude

In order to identify areas of sin that the Spirit is prompting you to address, make time in your schedule this week for solitude. Go to a park, on a hike, or for a drive by yourself. You know best how and where you experience solitude and peace from life's demands. Ask the Lord for wisdom. Seek to understand what the Lord wants you to change in your attitudes or actions. Use the space below to note your one or two main categories of sin as well as how you play out those categories in your life.

A Letter from Your Tempter

We all face temptation to sin every hour of every day. Sometimes the tempter is us, our self-centered flesh. Sometimes the tempter is the world around us: media images, cultural expectations, the "system" at work, and so on. And sometimes, the Bible tells us, the tempter is "the prince of this world" (John 12:31)—the Devil and his servants.

What if you could read the instructions a supervising demon gives your personal demon about how to tempt you? C. S. Lewis played out this "what-if" in his famous book *The Screwtape Letters*. Here's a sample from that book:

> My Dear Wormwood,
>   Let him assume that the first ardours of his conversion might have been expected to last, and ought to have lasted, forever, and that his present dryness is an equally permanent condition. Having once got this misconception well fixed in his head, you may then proceed in various ways. . . . You have only got to keep him out of the way of experienced Christians (an easy task nowadays), to direct his attention to the appropriate passages in Scripture, and then to set him to work on the desperate design of recovering his old feelings by sheer will power, and the game is ours. . . . If you can once get him to the point of thinking that "religion is all very well up to a point," you can feel quite happy about his soul. A moderated religion is as good for us as no religion at all—and more amusing.[4]

In the following exercise, you will write a fictional letter about yourself, as though a senior demon were instructing your personal demon in how to tempt you. The point is to get you thinking about how temptation and sin work in your life. What lies does the tempter feed you? In what situations are you most vulnerable to the tempter's voice? What sins do you frequently fall into or struggle with, and how does that occur?

As a believer, you are experiencing the Holy Spirit's transformation process. The Spirit opens your eyes to your sin, convicts you of it, and leads you to repentance. When you spend time in this kind of reflection, you become aware of the sin in your life. You realize that the Enemy loves to use whatever means possible to promote you to sin. Both your strengths and weaknesses can be twisted to sinfulness. For example, one of your strengths might be that you are a gifted encourager of other believers. How might your personal tempter twist this strength to make it an area of sin? Likewise, in an area of your weakness, perhaps pornography, what is your tempter's strategy? How does pornography rob you from experiencing joy in Christ?

Before you begin writing your letter, ask God to help you grow more godly and holy as a result of this reflection. Next, imagine a letter that your personal tempter's boss might write to your tempter about you and your vulnerabilities. Use the material you identified last week in the "Seven Deadly Sins" exercise to help identify your areas of greatest struggle. Think also of your strengths and how your tempter could render them ineffective. Knowing yourself the way you do, write as one wishing and plotting for your downfall. How would your tempter set you up to be rendered useless for the kingdom of God? How would he make use of your flesh and the world around you? Jot some notes.

Then choose one specific sin you struggle with, and write your letter about that. Your goal is to learn how to listen to the Holy Spirit's conviction and evaluate how sin affects your life. Your goal isn't to understand and write about every area you struggle with. If you cultivate an attitude of attentiveness to the Spirit of God and His conviction of sin in your life, you will experience a lifetime of growth in your struggle against sin. Therefore, choose only one area and try to clearly describe the dynamics of how your flesh, the world, and the Enemy tempt you in that area.

Think about yourself in practical terms. How does it happen that you are prone to react in anger toward your kids? How is it that you find yourself spreading gossip instead of remaining quiet? The letter ought to go beyond the behavior to the root of the sin. Why do you do it? What payoff do you get or expect to get? What lie are you falling for? What selfish motive makes you susceptible? Why do you let the world's pressure get to you in this area?

Be as transparent and vulnerable as you can appropriately be with your group. The more transparent you are, the more meaningful this exercise will be for you and them. Your group leader will probably have men and women separate into two subgroups when these letters are read, so you don't need to worry about material that you don't want to share with members of the opposite sex.

Also, confidentiality will be extremely important when these letters are read. The information in the letters must never be shared without permission, even to one's spouse. A breach of confidentiality in the group will often bring with it enormous tension, conflict, and loss of trust.

Try to keep your letter to one single-spaced page so everyone will have adequate time to share his or her letter. As a good rule of thumb, your letter will answer the following questions about your area of sin:

- When are you most susceptible to temptation in this area?
- What consequences can you associate with the sin?
- What payoff do you feel you get or might get from the sin? In other words, when you are tempted, what do you think you will gain or what benefit will you receive as a result of giving in?
- How do you tend to rationalize this area of sin? What does the reasoning process look like when you are rationalizing?

Spiritual Disciplines

Choose one spiritual discipline listed below or some other discipline that you have never consistently exercised. Exercise that discipline consistently throughout the coming week. During the week, think about how the discipline affects your dependence on God, and note your conclusions on page 100. Be prepared to discuss your experience of the exercise in the next session.

Practicing these disciplines is not a formula for sanctification, but it can be a great way to refocus your attention on God and others.

Types of Spiritual Disciplines

- *Scripture:* Reading, memorizing, meditating on verses
- *Prayer:* Praying silently, taking prayer walks, reading written prayers and liturgies
- *Fasting:* Abstaining from food to focus on God and prayer
- *Journaling:* Writing to God, tracking growth, expressing thoughts and feelings
- *Silence and solitude:* Taking time to be alone in absolute silence before God
- *Stewardship:* Managing your resources according to godly principles (for example, generous giving)
- *Service:* Finding opportunities to do acts of service for the benefit of others
- *Evangelism:* Sharing the gospel regularly through various means
- *Confession:* Confessing sin individually and in a group
- *Simplicity:* Limiting your lifestyle in order to free yourself for God
- *Worship:* Partaking in corporate and individual worship
- *Learning:* Reading, taking courses, participating in discussion groups
- *Meditation:* Contemplating biblical truth in order to better understand the character of God and its relevance to your own life
- *Fellowship:* Developing a partnership with other believers as an encouragement to your pursuit of personal holiness and corporate witness for Christ

Notes from the Spiritual Disciplines Exercise

The Fruit of the Spirit

In Galatians 5:22-23, Paul lists nine character qualities that comprise the fruit the Holy Spirit bears in a believer's life: love, joy, peace, patience, kindness, goodness, faithfulness, gentleness, and self-control. Read about each quality and respond to the questions about each. Identify friends, family members, and members of your small group who exhibit that quality.

Love

> *As pride can be seen as the root of all sin, love is the root of all godly deeds: Dear friends, let us love one another, for love comes from God. Everyone who loves has been born of God and knows God. Whoever does not love does not know God, because God is love. (1 John 4:7-8)*

Unfortunately, love often lacks the force it ought to have for believers because the English word *love* has lost much of its meaning as used in Scripture. People use the word in many ways to refer to a variety of sentiments expressed toward an even wider variety of objects. We have a critical need for our understanding of love to be biblically, rather than culturally, informed. However, cultivating love requires more than simply correcting our misunderstandings; it requires a personal reorientation.

Our world caters to our self-centeredness. Yet the love we find in Scripture, exemplified most profoundly in Christ's life, is an others-oriented love:

> *This is how we know what love is: Jesus Christ laid down his life for us. And we ought to lay down our lives for our brothers. If anyone has material possessions and sees his brother in need but has no pity on him, how can the love of God be in him? Dear children, let us not love with words or tongue but with actions and in truth. (1 John 3:16-18)*

If we are to cultivate love, we must learn to shift our focus from ourselves to those around us. None of us will fully rid ourselves of our ever-present preoccupation with self. And indeed, we benefit greatly from loving God and our neighbor. But cultivating love requires that we learn to love for the sake of the other rather than merely for our own benefit.

Biblical love is not just others-centered in our thinking but also in our actions. Love physically gives to others. It listens to those in pain and offers words of sympathy. It offers encouragement in the form of a smile. It gets its hands dirty helping a neighbor fix a car. In short, one who loves lays down self-interest for the interest of the other.

1. Do you currently have any relationships in which you love another for his or her sake, not just your own? How would you describe that relationship?

2. How do you seek to demonstrate others-oriented love in those relationships?

3. List those you know (including members of your group) who exhibit love. Describe how they demonstrate that characteristic.

4. How does observing love in those people spur you on to love similarly?

Joy

Those around us often understand happiness in terms of the absence of undesirable elements of life—pain, suffering, disappointment. In contrast, Christian joy is a response to the presence of something positive in our lives—the presence of Christ through the Spirit, along with the hope we have in Him. This presence and hope enable us to have joy in the midst of pain, suffering, and disappointment.

Joy comes from knowing that though we will experience the hardships that come with living in a fallen world, our present experience is nothing like the future that awaits us. As Karl Barth once said in the face of distress, Christian joy proclaims "a defiant 'Nevertheless!'"[5]

Even Christ's experience on the cross involved joy:

> *Let us fix our eyes on Jesus, the author and perfecter of our faith, who for the joy set before him endured the cross, scorning its shame, and sat down at the right hand of the throne of God. (Hebrews 12:2)*

Cultivating joy, like cultivating love, requires us to move beyond ourselves. We must move beyond our present circumstances, beyond our short-term pains and pleasures. Cultivating joy requires that we not pursue it as an end in itself but rather that we pursue God and one another in other-directed love. When we do so, we find that joy is a by-product. As John Stott writes, "The self-conscious pursuit of happiness will always end in failure. But when we forget ourselves in the self-giving sacrifice of love, then joy . . . comes flooding into our lives as an incidental, unlooked for blessing."[6]

> *Rejoice in the Lord always. I will say it again: Rejoice! Let your gentleness be evident to all. The Lord is near. (Philippians 4:4-5)*

When joy characterizes our lives, we aren't shaken by the tides of our circumstances. We still grieve during times of loss and rejoice in times of celebration. We're not stoic, lacking any expression of emotion. But we don't despair in times of loss, nor are we overly taken by temporal success. A joyful person has a strong awareness of God's good providence.

1. In what circumstances has a sense of joy been most evident in your life?

2. What circumstances most "steal" your joy?

3. How might others help you cultivate joy in your life?

4. List those you know (including members of your group) who exhibit
joy. Describe how they demonstrate it.

5. How does observing joy in those people spur you on to joy?

Peace

Our contemporary definition of peace can be misleading. We think of
peace as the absence of conflict, but Scripture gives a much richer perspective. Biblical peace involves total well-being, wholeness, and harmony.
Cultivating that kind of peace in our lives and relationships is hard in a
fragmented world like ours. A fallen world is full of obstacles to personal
wholeness, unity with our brothers and sisters, and justice in the world.
God has provided the way of ultimate reconciliation through Christ: "He
himself is our peace" (Ephesians 2:14). We can be agents of reconciliation
as we walk by the Spirit: "Blessed are the peacemakers, for they will be
called sons of God" (Matthew 5:9).

Though conflict is common in human relations and is necessary to a certain degree, it should not be an end in itself. Christians should aim not to be in conflict, either internally or interpersonally. Peacemakers pursue harmony in relationships. They aren't necessarily averse to conflict, but they want it to lead to resolution.

Internal peace comes from integrity. Peacemakers avoid living double lives. They seek to integrate areas of their lives. If possible, they want to work, go to church, and live in the same community, so as not to have unrelated sets of relationships. People characterized by peace are not secretive because they have nothing to hide.

1. What are some practical ways you can embody God's peace in your life context (for example, in your home, church, and community)?

2. How can you avoid acting as though your attitudes and actions in one area of life don't affect other areas? How can you avoid being a different person in different settings?

3. List those you know who exhibit peace internally and in relationships. Describe how they demonstrate it.

4. How does observing peace in those people spur you on to peace?

Patience

Be patient, then, brothers, until the Lord's coming. See how the farmer waits for the land to yield its valuable crop and how patient he is for the autumn and spring rains. You too, be patient and stand firm, because the Lord's coming is near. Don't grumble against each other, brothers, or you will be judged. The Judge is standing at the door!

Brothers, as an example of patience in the face of suffering, take the prophets who spoke in the name of the Lord. As you know, we consider blessed those who have persevered. You have heard of Job's persever- ance and have seen what the Lord finally brought about. The Lord is full of compassion and mercy. (James 5:7-11)

Time has become a commodity, and to some people, time is the most valuable commodity they have. We speak of spending time, saving time, wasting time, and buying time. Many professionals attend seminars that will teach them to invest their time wisely in order to get the greatest possible return on their investment. Yet in this world where we view time as a commodity and spend it expecting results, we are called to cultivate patience. Patience requires a willingness to lay aside our to-do lists and our incessant demands for quantifiable results for the sake of others' needs, our own spiritual development, and the worship of God. A patient person does not hoard time.

Another aspect of patience is restraint from taking matters into our own hands. Patient people, when circumstances necessitate, are willing to wait. They wait for clear direction from the Lord when confused about a job opportunity. They wait for a child to finish explaining an incident before rushing to judgment. They restrain their anger when their son embarrasses them in public. They wait for God's healing hand after the disappointing breakup of a relationship.

1. What circumstances consistently test your patience?

2. How do you typically react to those circumstances?

3. How might such circumstances help you cultivate patience?

4. How can you cultivate patience? How can others help you cultivate it?

5. List those you know who exhibit patience. Describe how they demonstrate it.

6. How does observing patience in those people spur you on to patience?

Kindness

When autonomy and self-sufficiency are cherished, little room is left for kindness. Philip Kenneson observes that "kindness is a particular manifestation of love's other-directedness. Kindness seems to manifest itself as a certain way of being helpful to those who need help. Such helpfulness stems first of all from God's helpfulness, of which the Christian is imminently mindful."[7]

For the self-sufficient individual, to seek such help is to admit one's inadequacy, and to be offered such help is an affront to one's sense of independence. Cultivating kindness involves the reciprocity of freely giving and receiving grace between needy people, not independence but interdependence. As with all of the Spirit's fruit, kindness is essentially an expression of other-directedness in that it calls us to be freely available to those around us.

In the parable of the good Samaritan, Jesus demonstrates the close connection between love and kindness. The Samaritan finds a victim of assault and robbery, personally bandages him, takes him to an inn, cares for him that evening, and then pays for his ongoing care. After telling the parable, Jesus vividly makes His point about the connection between love and kindness with a final question:

> *"Which of these three do you think was a neighbor to the man who fell into the hands of robbers?"*
> *The expert in the law replied, "The one who had mercy on him."*
> *Jesus told him, "Go and do likewise." (Luke 10:36-37)*

1. What keeps you from expressing kindness to others? What aspects of your culture, personality, or personal heritage (family and cultural background) hinder you?

2. List those you know who exhibit kindness. Describe how they demonstrate it.

3. How does observing kindness in those people spur you on to kindness?

Goodness

When the rich young ruler called Jesus "good teacher," Jesus reminded him that "no one is good—except God alone" (Mark 10:17-18). Like all of the Spirit's fruit, goodness is a reflection of God's character. However, many people in our time consider goodness to reside in the nature of humanity. What those people fail to recognize is that the only good inherent in humanity is what remains of the image of God placed in us at Creation (see Genesis 1:26-27). Goodness always has God as its source.

The London Times once asked a number of writers to submit essays on the topic "What's wrong with the world?" G. K. Chesterton's reply was the shortest and yet the most profound. His reply simply read, "Dear Sirs, I am. Sincerely, G. K. Chesterton."[8] Such an acute awareness of our fallenness leaves no room for the kind of self-affirmation and self-actualization prevalent in our society. John Stott affirms this truth:

> Christian believers are able to affirm only those aspects of the self which derive from our creation in God's image (e.g. our rational capacity, moral responsibility, and capacity for love), while at the same time denying (that is, disowning and repudiating) all those aspects of the self which derive from the fall and from our own personal fallenness. These Christian forms of self-affirmation and self-denial are very far from being expressions of a preoccupation, let alone an infatuation, with ourselves."[9]

We are not inherently good, but the Holy Spirit who indwells us is. Only through deferring to His power and presence in our lives can we develop the characteristic of goodness.

In John's gospel, Christ defines goodness by referring to Himself:

> *"I am the good shepherd. The good shepherd lays down his life for the sheep. The hired hand is not the shepherd who owns the sheep. So when he sees the wolf coming, he abandons the sheep and runs away. Then the wolf attacks the flock and scatters it." (John 10:11-12)*

In this passage, a good person not only avoids thinking maliciously about others but he also goes so far as to make personal sacrifices for them. Onlookers can see that a good person acts for others' well-being. Further, good people aren't fickle in their intentions. People don't say of the good woman, "She let us down, but she had good intentions." The good person follows through on good intentions.

1. In your mind, what qualifies a person as a "good person"?

2. If you consider yourself a "good person," in what sense do you think you are good?

3. List those you know who exhibit goodness. Describe how they demonstrate it.

4. How does observing goodness in those people spur you on to goodness?

Faithfulness

Few words come nearer to capturing God's character than the word *faithful*. All of salvation history testifies that God is a covenant-making and covenant-keeping God. In light of His unyielding faithfulness to His people, being called to imitate Him in this respect is an exceedingly high calling.

Cultivating faithfulness is difficult in a world like ours that downplays the significance of commitment and is obsessed with instant gratification. We must have what Eugene Peterson has called "a long obedience in the same direction."[10] Faithful husbands and wives keep their promises "until death do us part." Faithful students finish all their assignments on time. Faithful employees do not fudge on their work but rather press on diligently to complete a high-quality product. Faithful parents don't throw their hands up and give in to their children's disobedience; they continue to train and discipline them.

For Christians, faithfulness involves more than fulfilling one's commitments. It involves consistent dependence on God's power. The pages of Scripture are filled with tragic stories of men and women who sought to chart their own course rather than remain steadfast in following God's direction. The entire history of Israel demonstrates that when memory grows short, commitment and dependence grow weak. Our faithfulness to God in the present requires a profound appreciation of His faithfulness to us in the past and an unreserved confidence in His promises for the future.

1. What are some of the most significant ways God has demonstrated His faithfulness to you?

2. What are some of God's faithful acts that you often forget to be thankful for?

3. In what areas do you struggle the most with being faithful to your commitments?

4. How can others help you cultivate consistency to follow through with your responsibilities?

5. List those you know who exhibit faithfulness. Describe how they demonstrate it.

6. How does observing faithfulness in those people spur you on to faithfulness?

Gentleness

All of our lives are, to some degree, ambition-driven. We want to be significant and have our lives count for something. These desires aren't necessarily evil, but if left unchecked, they can choke out the fruit of gentleness. In a world where those who wield power are the ones who make a difference, ambition-driven Christians can easily give in to the seduction of power.

Our culture tells us, "If you want to get anything done . . . if you want to make an impact, you have to be in a position of power to do so; otherwise, you are doomed to ineffectiveness, and ultimately, failure. Hence, people who want to make their mark on the world will have to make peace with doing so by using the world's ways, which are usually the ways of power and coercion."[11]

Gentleness, meekness, and humility involve "the strength to refrain from power and coercion."[12] Those who are gentle are not the opposite of those who are strong. They simply refrain from using their strength for intimidation or manipulation. They realize that by being gentle, they can encourage and edify another. A gentle person is one by whom others don't feel threatened when they're vulnerable. They will reveal their fears and confusion because they know that this gentle person does not inflict pain on those who are vulnerable.

If someone tells about his demotion at work, the gentle man does not accuse the person of poor performance. ("Well, you must not have worked hard enough.") The gentle woman does not condemn her friend who admits to hitting her child in a moment of anger. ("How dare you do such a thing!") The gentle person will try to channel personal strength toward helping others, not condemning them.

1. Can Christians be ambitious and at the same time cultivate gentleness? If so, how? If not, why not?

2. How does an initial response of gentleness rather than correction communicate love to someone who reveals a failure or sin?

3. How does that initial gentleness provide a platform for later influence in the person's life that can lead to repentance?

4. List those you know who exhibit gentleness. Describe how they demonstrate it.

5. How does observing gentleness in those people spur you on to gentleness?

Self-Control

The final quality mentioned in Paul's list of the Spirit's fruit may seem out of place. The others share a common theme of other-centeredness. Yet at the conclusion of the list we find what most translations call *self*-control.

In the Greek world of Paul's day, self-control was a chief virtue, foundational to developing all other virtues. If one was to master the virtuous life, he first must learn to master his own emotions and desires; he must learn to be controlled by nothing. Yet when Paul identified this virtue as a fruit of the Spirit, he used the term differently from the way others used it. In calling self-control a fruit of the Spirit, Paul attributed the control of the self not to the individual's work but to the Spirit's work in that individual's life. For Paul, self-control meant to be controlled by God.

When we understand self-control in this way, we see that perhaps the best way we can cultivate this fruit is not necessarily through more concentrated efforts of our will. Instead, we should do what we can to nourish the other aspects of the Spirit's fruit, all of which call us to forget ourselves in the service of others and in the worship and service of God.

1. In what areas do you struggle to control desires or emotions?

2. How can others help you cultivate control over those areas?

3. List those you know who exhibit self-control. Describe how they demonstrate it.

4. How does observing self-control in those people spur you on to having self-control?

Spiritual Discipline Exercise — Worship

Take some time this week for worship. The fruit of the Spirit is merely a reflection of God's glory in our lives. As you contemplate the fruit of the Spirit, remember that those characteristics don't originate in us but in our glorious Creator and Savior. Set aside a time in which you focus not on your current circumstances or personal relationships or the tasks on your schedule but upon the character of God. Express your appreciation for His continuing work of sanctifying you.

Leader's Guide

Introduction

This leader's guide will:
- Explain the intended purpose of each session and how each session fits into the entire study
- Provide you with plenty of discussion questions so that you can choose a few that suit your group
- Suggest other ways of interacting over the material

The first step in leading this study is to read "A Model of Spiritual Transformation" beginning on page 7. The section describes three broad approaches to growth and explains how the four studies in the series fit together.

There's more involved in leading a small group, however, than just understanding the study and its objective. The main skill you'll need is creating a group environment that facilitates authentic interaction among people. Every leader does this in his or her own style, but here are two principles necessary for all:

1. *Avoid the temptation to speak whenever people don't immediately respond to one of your questions.* As the leader, you may feel pressure to break the silence. Often, though, leaders overestimate how much silence has gone by. Several seconds of silence may seem like a minute to the leader. However, usually people just need time to collect their thoughts before they respond. If you wait patiently for their responses, they will usually take that to mean you really do want them to say what they think. On the other hand, if you consistently break the silence yourself, they may not feel the need to speak up.

2. *Avoid being a problem solver.* If you immediately try to solve every problem that group members voice, they won't feel comfortable sharing issues of personal struggle. Why? Because most people,

when sharing their problems, initially want to receive acceptance and empathy rather than advice. They want others to understand and care about the troubled state of their soul. Giving immediate advice can often communicate that you feel they are not bright enough to figure out the solution.

Getting a Small Group Started

You may be gathering a group of friends to do a study together or possibly you've volunteered to lead a group that your church is assembling. Regardless of the circumstances, God has identified you as the leader.

You are probably a peer of the other group members. Some may have read more theology than you, some may have more church ministry experience than you, and yet God has providentially chosen you as the leader. You're not the "teacher" or the sole possessor of wisdom—you are simply responsible to create an atmosphere that facilitates genuine interaction.

One of the most effective ways you can serve your group is to *make clear what is expected*. You are the person who informs group members. They need to know, for example, where and when your first meeting will be held. If you're meeting in a home and members need maps, make sure they receive them in a timely manner. If members don't have study books, help them each obtain one. To create a hospitable setting for your meetings, you will need to plan for refreshments or delegate that responsibility to others. A group phone and e-mail list may also be helpful; ask the group if it's okay to distribute their contact information to one another. Make sure there's a sense of order. You may even want to chart out a tentative schedule of all the sessions, including any off weeks for holidays.

The first several sessions are particularly important because they are when you will communicate your vision for the group. You'll want to explain your vision several times during your first several meetings. Many people need to hear it several times before it really sinks in, and some will probably miss the first meeting or two. Communicate your vision and expectations concisely so that plenty of time remains for group discussion. People will drop out if the first session feels like a monologue from the leader.

One valuable thing to do in this first meeting is to let group members tell a brief history of themselves. This could involve a handful of facts about where they come from and how they ended up in this group.

Also, in your first or second meeting, ask group members to share their expectations. The discussion may take the greater part of a meeting, but it's worth the time invested because it will help you understand each person's perspective. Here are some questions for initiating a discussion of group members' expectations:

• How well do you expect to get to know others in the group?
• Describe your previous experiences with small groups. Do you expect this group to be similar or different?
• What do you hope the group will be like by the time the study ends?
• How do you think this group will contribute to your walk with Christ?
• Do you need to finish the meeting by a certain time, or do you prefer open-ended meetings? Do you expect to complete this study in eleven sessions, or will you be happy extending it by a few sessions if the additional time serves your other goals for the group?

If you have an extended discussion of people's expectations, you probably won't actually begin session 1 of this study guide until the second time you meet. This is more likely if your group is just forming than if your group has been together for some time. By the time you start the first session in the study guide, group members ought to be accustomed to interacting with one another. This early investment will pay big dividends. If you plan to take a whole meeting (or even two) to lay this kind of groundwork, be sure to tell the group what you're doing and why. Otherwise, some people may think you're simply inefficient and unable to keep the group moving forward.

Remember that many people will feel nervous during the first meeting. This is natural; don't feel threatened by it. Your attitude and demeanor will set the tone. If you are passive, the group will lack direction and vision. If you are all business and no play, they will expect that the group will have a formal atmosphere, and you will struggle to get people to lighten up. If you are all play and no business, they will expect the group to be all fluff and won't take it seriously. Allow the group some time and freedom to form a "personality." If many group members enjoy a certain activity, join in with them. Don't try to conform the group to your interests. You may have to be willing to explore new activities.

What does the group need from you initially as the leader?

- *Approachability:* Be friendly, ask questions, avoid dominating the discussion, engage with group members before and after the sessions, allow group members opportunities to ask you questions too.

- *Connections:* Pay attention to how you can facilitate bonding. (For example, if you learn in separate conversations that two group members, Joe and Tom, went to State University, you might say, "Joe, did you know that Tom also went to State U?")

- *Communication of Logistics:* Be simple, clear, and concise. (For instance, be clear about what will be involved in the group sessions, how long they will last, and where and when they will occur.)

- *Summary of Your Leadership Style:* You might want to put together some thoughts about your style of leadership and be prepared to share them with the group. You might include such issues as:

  1. The degree of flexibility with which you operate (for example, your willingness to go on "rabbit trails" versus staying on topic)

  2. Your level of commitment to having prayer or worship as a part of the group

  3. Your attentiveness, or lack thereof, to logistics (making sure to discuss the details surrounding your group, such as when and where you are meeting, or how to maintain communication with one another if something comes up)

  4. The degree to which you wear your emotions on your sleeve

  5. Any aspects of your personality that have often been misunderstood (for instance, "People sometimes think that I'm not interested in what they are saying because I don't immediately respond, when really I'm just pondering what they were saying.")

  6. Any weaknesses you are aware of as a leader (for example, "Because I can tend to dominate the group by talking too much, I will appreciate anybody letting me know if I am doing so." Or, "I get very

engaged in discussion and can consequently lose track of time, so I may need you to help me keep on task so we finish on time.")

7. How you plan to address any concerns you have with group members (for instance, "If I have concerns about the way anyone is interacting in the group, perhaps by consistently offending another group member, I will set up time to get together and address it with that person face-to-face.")

- *People Development:* Allow group members to exercise their spiritual gifts. See their development not as a threat to your leadership but as a sign of your success as a leader. For instance, if group members enjoy worshiping together and you have someone who can lead the group in worship, encourage that person to do so. However, give direction in this so that the person knows exactly what you expect. Make sure he or she understands how much worship time you want.

Beginning the Sessions

Before you jump into session 1, make sure that group members have had a chance to read "A Model of Spiritual Transformation" beginning on page 7 and "A Method for the Biblical Exercises" beginning on page 15. Also, ask if they have done what is listed in the "Preparation" section of session 1. Emphasize that the assignments for each session are as important as the group meetings and that inadequate preparation for a session diminishes the whole group's experience.

Overview of *Integrity*

The average Christian has learned how to be nice, polite, and pleasant to others and has discovered (perhaps unconsciously) that these qualities often pass for Christlike character. Some Christians also have learned some skills, such as Bible study and quiet time methods, that can contribute to spiritual growth. However, the challenge of the Christian life is not merely to change behavior but to experience true, deep life change at the heart level. How does that happen in practical terms, especially in those areas of our lives where specific sin issues hold us back?

This study focuses on two objectives. In the first half of the study, group members will focus upon the effects of sin in a believer's life. The study helps group members not only identify which particular sin issues they struggle with but also share those sin issues with others. The process of identification and confession is critical for the believer's resistance to sin. The Spirit of God guides this process, helping a believer identify sin issues that He desires to address. Those issues are identified both privately (through prayer, study of the Word, or spiritual promptings) and publicly (by His ministry through others' feedback). The first focal point, then, is helping group members identify sin issues and employ the support of God and the community of believers.

The second objective is to help group members focus on positive growth toward holiness. This objective moves beyond the defensive posture of resisting sin to the offensive posture of learning to live with deeper love and more conscientious conduct. Group members will identify areas for growth and seek the support of God and other believers.

Life Change

To help your group attain the study's objectives, you will use a tool called "Life Change." This tool provides exercises for group members to complete in preparation for the sessions. "Life Change" is located on pages 73-121. The "Life Change" exercises are critical in helping members identify areas of struggle and areas for growth.

Life change happens best in community. We need each other's help. We must learn to approach each other without a defensive superficiality. We need courage to move beyond our comfort zones, open our lives, and be involved in each other's life-change process. Then we are on the road to fulfilling Christ's new command: to love each other as He has loved us (see John 13:34-35). No one can guarantee that courageous love will occur in your group. We can only trust God to create it, and we invite you, as the leader, to risk being authentic within your group.

The Order of Sessions

The first few sessions will introduce the topic of integrity, helping group members see that integrity is not merely the result of having biblical knowledge or exercising private disciplines. Christian integrity requires public application of biblical truth together with other believers.

Sessions 3–6 provide a context for group members to identify and share with the group the personal dynamics of sin in one area of their lives. Session 7, "The Fear of the Lord," acts as a transition into the discussion of positive growth toward holiness. Sessions 8–10 address that growth process. Session 11 offers a conclusion to the study by having group members consider how they will pursue growth in integrity for their entire lives, not just for one season of life.

Discussion Questions

This "Leader's Guide" contains questions that we think will help you attain the goal of each session and build community in your group. Use our discussion questions in addition to the ones you come up with on your own, but don't feel pressured to use all of them. However, we think it's wise to use some of them. If one question is not a good vehicle for discussion, then use another. It can be helpful to rephrase the questions in your own words.

Session 1: Christian Integrity and Community

We hope you have had a chance to get the group together before you meet to discuss session 1. If so, group members should have had the chance to read the session and do the biblical exercise beginning on page 19. You may want to begin the session by addressing people's expectations for the study. This topic can be intimidating for many people and downright frightening for others. To share one's struggles with sin will not be an easy process for most group members. You may choose to begin with the following two questions or ones similar to these:

1. What are your expectations for this study?

2. What are your fears about addressing issues of personal sin and areas for growth in the context of a group?

To discuss the content of the session, select several of the following questions or come up with your own. The point of this session is to get people to see the importance of others in their own growth.

1. Do you typically think of growing in holiness and righteousness as a private endeavor or a communal one? Why do you think that you have such a view of growth?

2. What does Ephesians 4 say about the corporate nature of Christian growth and life change?

3. In what sense is growth an issue of personal responsibility? In what sense is it an issue of allowing the power of God to change us? In what sense is it an issue of receiving the support of a group of other believers?

4. Can you give an example from personal experience in which all three components of growth (personal responsibility, the power of God, and help from others) played a part?

As you close the first session, make sure the group is clear about how to complete the "Belief and Practice" exercise in "Life Change." Remind them to be prepared at your next meeting to share some of their observations from the experience.

Session 2: Belief and Practice

The goal of this session is to help group members see that life change is not accomplished merely by knowing the right things. Knowledge is not a substitute for a long-term, committed pursuit of holiness. While our beliefs may be biblically accurate, they are not consistently exhibited in our daily lives. In order to make this point clear, much of the discussion revolves around having the group share examples of how they have experienced change in the past—how they came to believe and practice a biblical principle.

To introduce the session, select one or two questions from below. However, devote the majority of the session to letting group members share the results of their "Life Change" exercise.

1. Have you ever felt oppressed after hearing a sermon or reading a book about principles of Christian living?

2. Did that have an effect on your willingness to be honest about your failure to live up to the ideal Christian life as you understood it? In other words, were you tempted to create a facade of godliness even if your heart was not in it?

3. Name something that you believe but is not evident in your life. (For instance, someone might believe a Christian should be "anxious for nothing" but then panic whenever bill-paying time comes.)

4. In what ways can we individually bridge the gap between belief and practice? How can we privately depend on God's power? (Possible responses: time in the Word, in prayer, in exercising other spiritual disciplines.)

5. How can a commitment with others help bridge the gap? How can we depend on God's power for growth as a result of community? (Possible responses: relationships of accountability and encouragement, reminding one another of commitments to growth.)

Shift into a time of sharing from the "Life Change" exercise. Begin the sharing time by stating something like this:

> Now let's take some time to share what we recorded in the "Life Change" exercise. Share with the group one of the biblical principles you noted, and talk about what factors had a role in your coming to believe and practice it in your daily life—for example, time in the Word, encouragement from others, personal will and choices, dependence on God through prayer.

After the sharing time, point out the diverse manner in which group members experienced change. Ask the group the following question:

1. What were the various factors involved in the stories of growth we just shared with one another? Are there any commonalities?

Leave time for members in your group to pray for each other. Life change will happen only as the Spirit works, and we should ask Him to move in our midst.

Session 3: Flesh

In this session, you want group members to face their own propensity to choose sinful actions and attitudes. While there are certainly factors that influence each of us to sin, we are individually responsible for choosing to act or think sinfully. Discuss some of the following questions:

1. What does Romans 1 say about our individual responsibility for sin?

2. How does Paul address any excuses we make for our sin?

3. Can you give examples from the present that are similar or related to the sin issues Paul cited in Romans? How do these present issues affect you?

4. In Galatians 5:19-21 (NET), Paul identifies the "works of the flesh" as "sexual immorality, impurity, depravity, idolatry, sorcery, hostilities, strife, jealousy, outbursts of anger, selfish rivalries, dissensions, factions, envying, murder, drunkenness, carousing, and similar things." How do these reflect an outlook oriented toward the self? (For instance, what are the self-serving motivations that underlie immorality, impurity, sensuality, and so on?)

5. These overt manifestations of the flesh can be summed up by two broad categories of motivation: the desire for control and power ("What can I do?") and the desire for selfish gratification ("What can I get?"). How do these motives work out in more subtle ways in your life contexts (such as your workplace, family, and church)?

6. If the flesh is "the outlook oriented toward the self," what resources do we Christians have (Scripture, for example) to help us overcome this orientation? How can we take advantage of those resources?

Make sure the group is aware of the "Seven Deadly Sins" exercise to be completed for the next session.

Session 4: Seven Deadly Sins

This session and the next two could be critical points for your group's progression through this study. In this session, you will begin to prepare for the exercise called "A Letter from Your Tempter," in which group members will write what their experience with sin is like. In sessions 5 and 6, group members will share their letters with one another.

Use the following questions to help members open up. Do not pry into every area, and be sensitive to members' fear of sharing. The exercise next week will cover many of these issues at a more personal level. Pray for your group as you open the sharing. Your honesty and vulnerability as the leader will set the tone for the group.

If you have a mixed-gender group, it might be wise to separate into same-sex discussion groups for sessions 4 through 6. Choose someone of the opposite sex to lead the second group. Use the following questions or come up with your own:

1. How do you feel about revealing areas of sin and struggle in your life? How do you want others to respond to you when you do so? What is your greatest fear about how others might respond?

2. Do you think revealing areas of struggle with sin can be a positive experience? If so, how? If not, why not?

3. What was your reaction to the descriptions of the seven deadly sins?

4. How difficult was it for you to determine your one or two most prevalent issues of sin?

5. Would other people who know you fairly well identify those same sin issues for you? Why, or why not? Is anyone besides you aware of those current areas of struggle?

6. Are the one or two most prevalent sins in your life recent struggles, or have you struggled with them for a long time?

7. Can the main sin in your life change depending on your life circumstances? What life circumstances cause you to struggle more with one area than with another?

Take some time at the end of the session to explain the "Life Change" exercise called "A Letter from Your Tempter." As the leader, you should be quite familiar with the exercise and able to answer questions about how to write the letter. Before the end of the session, make sure to indicate who will be sharing their tempter letters in the next session so those persons can be prepared.

Sessions 5 and 6: A Letter from Your Tempter

Each person will read his or her tempter letter over the course of two sessions. You should decide whether you will read your letter first or ask for a volunteer to go first.

The advantage of reading yours first is that you give the group an example of how to vulnerably share sin issues. The disadvantage is that you have no control or influence over how the group responds to your letter. It's ideal to have a trusted group member share his or her letter first so that you can lead the group's response to that first letter.

The response to these letters is of critical importance. Because this is a form of confession, group members need to listen carefully and compassionately. Lead the response by asking if there is any way that the group members can support the person who shared. Allow group members to respond by asking follow-up questions or offering appreciation to the reader for sharing. Most important, take time after each letter to pray for the reader.

Provide a good model for asking helpful follow-up questions. For example, "You said that the sin seems to provide you with an escape from reality. What in your life are you seeking to escape from?" If the reader is too ambiguous about his or her struggle with sin, the following questions can help. However, use them with caution. If the group member is uncomfortable revealing specific details about sin issues, don't try to force vulnerability. Such attempts will destroy any trust you have established.

1. How has your sin manifested itself recently?

2. When are you most susceptible to temptation in these areas?

3. What kind of consequences can you associate with your sin?

Finish each session with two emphases: First, encourage group members to support and pray for each other regarding their struggles with sin; second, remind the group that confession is only one part of growth and that the rest of the study will focus on positive growth in holiness.

Session 7: The Fear of the Lord

This session provides a transition into the latter half of the study with its emphasis on growing in holiness. Growing in integrity is more than simply avoiding sin. We are called to actively pursue holiness. Having an appropriate fear of the Lord not only helps us resist sin but it also motivates us to pursue growth. You want group members to consider how they maintain a healthy fear of the Lord. See Acts 9:31 for an example of the fear of the Lord in the New Testament church.

In your meeting, review the two stories from Genesis chapters 20 and 22, and then facilitate the conversation with the following questions:

1. How is Abraham's fear of men connected with his fear of God in Genesis 20?

2. In what ways do you not identify with Abraham's fear of God in Genesis 22? In what ways do you identify with it?

3. How might we tend to act as if God is malicious?

4. How might we tend to act as if He is permissive?

5. Does our culture hinder us from cultivating appropriate reverence for God's authority? If so, how?

6. How do we live as children under grace while maintaining fear of the Lord?

7. How does your reverence for God affect your attempt to guard against the areas of struggle you discussed in previous sessions?

8. How do you deal with the inevitable tension of fearing God and also having an intimate love relationship with Him?

9. Are you growing in the fear of the Lord? What contributes to your growth in this area? What keeps you from experiencing more growth?

10. How can we as a community contribute to your growth in the fear of the Lord?

Session 8: Spirit

The issue for group members to wrestle with is what walking in the Spirit looks like in daily life. How does someone depend on the Spirit of God as he or she pursues holiness? Consider asking the following:

1. What did you learn about the Spirit's role in the Christian life from John 15 and 16? What struck you in your study of those passages?

2. What role does the Spirit play in your growth in contrast to the role you play?

3. Have you experienced times in your life when you depersonalized God? If so, what led you to that point, and what made you aware of it?

4. When we find ourselves having depersonalized God and struggling to relate to Him, how can our situation improve?

5. Have you ever had a "formula" for how to walk by the Spirit? How have such formulas been helpful, and how have they been deficient?

6. As you understand it, what does it mean to "walk by the Spirit"?

7. In defining life in the Spirit, we have used such words as *dependence* and *surrender*. What do these concepts look like in our day-to-day lives?

8. In seeking to live a life of complete surrender to the Spirit, what criteria should we use to evaluate what He wants us to do?

9. How have you been doing at living out the life of the Spirit? What has helped you? What has held you back?

Remind group members of the "Spiritual Disciplines" exercise for next week. Let them know that you will want them to share what they learn from the exercise.

Session 9: Spiritual Disciplines

Begin the session by having group members share about the "Spiritual Disciplines" exercise from "Life Change." You can use the following questions to initiate discussion after the sharing:

1. Describe your experience with the "Spiritual Disciplines" exercise. How did it affect your daily endeavor to walk by the Spirit? How were you made more aware of others? How did it affect your ability to serve and love others?

2. How do your current life circumstances affect your exercising of spiritual disciplines? What about your lifestyle hinders it? What helps it?

3. Would you consider yourself a disciplined person by nature?

4. Which is or would be the most difficult spiritual discipline for you? Why?

5. If you were to exercise that discipline, how do you think it would benefit your relationship with Christ?

6. Which of the disciplines listed on page 99 do you practice or have you practiced regularly? Describe the impact of each discipline on your moment-by-moment dependence on God.

7. Which of the disciplines listed on page 99 have you never practiced at all? How might one of those disciplines affect your pursuit of holiness?

8. Which pitfall—legalism or passivity—are you more likely to fall into? What helps you avoid that pitfall?

9. How do personality type and temperament affect one's approach to spiritual disciplines?

10. How do you think your personality contributes to a proper or improper exercise of spiritual disciplines?

Make sure the group understands the "Fruit of the Spirit" exercise and comes ready to share next week.

Session 10: The Fruit of the Spirit

Facilitate a conversation in which group members relay what aspects of the fruit of the Spirit they see in one another's lives. Simply open up discussion by saying something like, "After going through the 'Fruit of the Spirit' exercise, how do you see those characteristics in the lives of other group members?" Let members be silent for a while if they're reluctant to be the first to share. If no one starts after a lengthy silence, you should be prepared to share some of your own observations about fruit in group members' lives. Also, have group members respond to the following questions after the sharing time:

1. In what areas of your life are you struggling to cultivate the fruit of the Spirit? In what areas of your life are you seeing growth of the Spirit's fruit most prominently?

2. What characteristics of the Spirit's fruit do you try to develop in your own life?

3. How can the presence of Christian community in your life help you cultivate the fruit?

4. How can exercising a spiritual discipline help you bear fruit?

Session 11: Growing in Integrity

In this session, you want to emphasize that the purpose of this study is not just growing in integrity for a few months but for the rest of your lives. Use the following questions to help group members think through their perspective on growth as a lifelong endeavor:

1. How would you describe the season of life you are in right now?

2. What are some unique challenges in this season of your life?

3. Have any of those challenges caused you to struggle in an area in which you previously considered yourself to be strong? If so, how?

4. What unique opportunities for growth does this season provide?

5. Describe an experience in your life in which you faced the temptation to sin in an area you had previously experienced growth.

6. How has God used a failure in a particular season of life to cause you to grow?

7. What lessons from previous seasons do you find most useful in your current season?

8. What lessons are you learning in this season that you think will be particularly important in future seasons?

9. How would having a view of yourself and your Christian maturity that is too high affect your ability to grow in integrity over a lifetime?

10. How would a view of yourself that is too low affect your ability to grow in integrity over a lifetime?

11. In what ways might you experience new challenges to your integrity as a result of taking on new roles or entering new life stages? (For example, getting married, having children, facing an empty nest.)

12. How does having to relate with certain types of personalities uniquely challenge you in certain areas of integrity? (For instance, you might be tempted to gossip when you have to work with someone who tends to gossip.)

As you wrap up this session, leave about fifteen minutes for group members to express what they have learned from this study. Doing so will help solidify the lessons they have learned. You might ask something like, "How has this study had an impact on your spiritual life? What have you learned or relearned as a result of it? What do you want to take with you from this study?"

Conclusion

We hope this study has been helpful for you and your group members. We desire to provide materials that help believers grow in Christ through small-group communities. Don't hesitate to contact us if you have any questions!

Phone: (214) 841-3515
E-mail: sf@dts.edu

Notes

A Method for the Biblical Exercises

1. Howard G. Hendricks and William D. Hendricks, *Living By the Book* (Chicago: Moody, 1991), p. 166.

Session 1: Christian Integrity and Community

1. Anthony A. Hoekema, *Saved by Grace* (Grand Rapids, Mich.: Eerdmans, 1989), p. 229.
2. Edmund Clowney, *The Church: Contours of Christian Theology* (Downers Grove, Ill.: InterVarsity, 1995), p. 89.

Session 2: Belief and Practice

1. "integrity," *Webster's Encyclopedic Unabridged Dictionary of the English Language* (New York: Gramercy Books, 1996), p. 738.
2. C. S. Lewis, *The Abolition of Man* (New York: Macmillan, 1965), p. 35.

Session 3: Flesh

1. Dallas Willard, *The Divine Conspiracy: Rediscovering Your Hidden Life in God* (San Francisco: HarperSanFrancisco, 1998), p. 38.
2. Scot McKnight, *Galatians* (Grand Rapids, Mich.: Zondervan, 1995), p. 266.
3. Robert Pyne, *Humanity and Sin: The Creation, Fall, and Redemption of Humanity* (Nashville: Word, 1999), p. 187. The preceding paragraph draws heavily upon the ideas expressed by Dr. Pyne in his lectures on anthropology.
4. Anthony C. Thiselton, "flesh," *New International Dictionary of New Testament Theology*, ed. Colin Brown (Grand Rapids, Mich.: Zondervan, 1986), 1:680.

Session 4: Seven Deadly Sins

1. John of the Cross, "Excerpts from *The Dark Night of the Soul*" in
   Devotional Classics: Selected Readings for Individuals and Groups, ed.
   Richard J. Foster and James Bryan Smith (San Francisco:
   HarperSanFrancisco, 1993), p. 36.
2. Dante Alighieri, *The Divine Comedy: Inferno*, trans. Allen Mandelbaum
   (New York: Bantam Books, 1982), p. 61.

Session 7: The Fear of the Lord

1. Craig Blaising, "Spirituality and Academics" (chapel message, Dallas
   Theological Seminary, Dallas, 1982).

Session 8: Spirit

1. Daniel Wallace, "Who's Afraid of the Holy Spirit? The Uneasy Conscience
   of a Noncharismatic Evangelical," *Christianity Today* (September 12,
   1994), pp. 36-37.
2. Anthony C. Thiselton, "flesh," *New International Dictionary of New
   Testament Theology*, ed. Colin Brown (Grand Rapids, Mich.:
   Zondervan, 1986), 1:680.
3. Scot McKnight, *Galatians* (Grand Rapids, Mich.: Zondervan, 1995), p. 269.

Session 9: Spiritual Discipline

1. Jonathan Edwards, *Jonathan Edwards: Representative Selections, with
   Introduction, Bibliography, and Notes*, ed. Clarence H. Faust and
   Thomas H. Johnson (New York: Hill and Wang, 1962), p. 38.
2. Edwards, p. 43.
3. Donald S. Whitney, *Spiritual Disciplines for the Christian Life* (Colorado
   Springs, Colo.: NavPress, 1991), p. 15.
4. R. Kent Hughes, *Disciplines of a Godly Man* (Wheaton, Ill.: Crossway,
   2001), p. 206.
5. Dallas Willard, *Hearing God: Developing a Conversational Relationship with
   God* (Downers Grove, Ill.: InterVarsity, 1999), p. 194.
6. Richard J. Foster, *Celebration of Discipline: The Path to Spiritual Growth*
   (San Francisco: HarperSanFrancisco, 1978), p. 6.
7. Foster, p. 6.

Session 10: The Fruit of the Spirit

1. Philip D. Kenneson, *Life on the Vine: Cultivating the Fruit of the Spirit in Christian Community* (Downers Grove, Ill.: InterVarsity, 1999), pp. 18-19.

Life Change

1. Definitions attributed to Kaye Briscoe King, a Christian counselor, are from her unpublished manuscript and are used by permission.
2. William Backus, *What Your Counselor Never Told You: Seven Secrets Revealed; Conquer the Power of Sin in Your Life* (Minneapolis: Bethany, 2000), p. 125.
3. Søren Kierkegaard, *Either/Or: A Fragment of a Life*, ed. Victor Eremita, trans. Alastair Hannay (New York: Penguin, 1992).
4. C. S. Lewis, *The Screwtape Letters* (New York: Macmillan, 1959), pp. 42-43.
5. Karl Barth, *Epistle to the Philippians* (Richmond, Va.: John Knox Press, 1962), p. 120.
6. John Stott, *The Contemporary Christian: Applying God's Word to Today's World* (Downers Grove, Ill.: InterVarsity, 1992), pp. 150-151.
7. Philip D. Kenneson, *Life on the Vine: Cultivating the Fruit of the Spirit in Christian Community* (Downers Grove, Ill.: InterVarsity, 1999), p. 136.
8. Philip Yancey, introduction to *Orthodoxy*, by G. K. Chesterton (Wheaton, Ill.: Harold Shaw Publishers, 1994), p. xii.
9. Stott, p. 150.
10. Eugene H. Peterson, *A Long Obedience in the Same Direction: Discipleship in an Instant Society* (Downers Grove, Ill.: InterVarsity, 1980).
11. Kenneson, p. 210.
12. Kenneson, p. 205.

OTHER BOOKS IN THE TRANSFORMING LIFE SERIES.

Identity
Pinpoint key elements of who you are—your heritage, roles, and distinctiveness—in Christ.
1-57683-558-8

Community
Explore what it takes to combat isolation and build true Christian community.
1-57683-559-6

Ministry
Your interests, struggles, and talents can help you discern how God has uniquely designed you to serve. This study will help you find your unique niche in the body of Christ.
1-57683-562-6

To get your copies, visit your local bookstore, call 1-800-366-7788, or log on to www.navpress.com. Ask for a FREE catalog of NavPress products. Offer BPA.

BRINGING TRUTH TO LIFE
www.navpress.com